WHAT
TEENS
SAY

A Report to Parents and Church Youth Workers on What Young People Are Saying and a Guide to Dealing with Questions These Young People Are Raising.

By Verna Joiner

THE WARNER PRESS   **ANDERSON, INDIANA**

COPYRIGHT ©, 1962, BY GOSPEL TRUMPET COMPANY

ALL RIGHTS RESERVED

Library of Congress Catalog Card No. 62-20181

PRINTED IN THE UNITED STATES OF AMERICA

A FOREWORD TO PARENTS AND TEACHERS

"I don't dare tell my mother; heaven only knows what she would do." These were the very words of a girl not quite fourteen. And from a boy not much older: "What can a teen-age boy do when his father is against him in everything, no matter how hard he tries to please?"

What are your teens saying—or if they are too conscientious or shy to talk, what do they think about their parents? Do they look upon them as people who care above all others what happens to them? One girl wrote me, "I like my family very well, but I do wish my parents would be a little more understanding."

Are you the parents? Did these letters come from your homes? "My dad never has a kind word for Mom, and the way he treats me—I've been thinking of running away from home—but where can I go?" "Mom won't believe me; when I try to explain, she slaps me and says I'm only making excuses." "My father knows the Bible and talks a lot about religion, but he doesn't live it . . ." "My parents are very sweet and understanding but . . ." "Please help me to find God!"

Are you the church school teacher? the youth leader? the pastor of scores of fellows and girls who are seeking for a real assurance of salvation? Some are too shy to go to a public altar or to ask for personal counsel, some are confused about which church is right, some are uncertain about the way to salvation, and some fear that their sin is too great. Countless teens, having failed to measure to standards, suffer from criticism of adults and guilt of conscience. They hunger for a satisfying experience—approval of God and the church—yet know not how to attain it.

Many of these have no spiritual resources at home. Do they find help in your class? in Youth Fellowship? in regular church services? Do you seek them out in personal friendly relationships—invite their confidence by showing love and concern? Do you visit them in their homes and make them welcome at your house?

Are the adult Christians your young people know overly dogmatic about relatively minor matters of Christian outlook and behavior? When teens overstep Christian standards, are you quick to condemn, perhaps publicly? Is the atmosphere of your church that of genuine love and concern?

Are you the church on Main Street, the popular church which says by attitude and example: "We want to be as much like the world as possible. We must adjust our gospel to the customs of our day—the age we're living in"? Are you saying the New Testament is no longer workable?

Young adults are expressing anxiety over these different and conflicting standards. They feel the need of a general group conscience about such things as dancing, movies, and dress. They would like more help on the art of dating and expressing affection. Just what do we expect of them? All too often they do not know. Do we?

How can we as parents and church leaders provide the *guidance* and *restraint* youth ask for and need? How can we utilize and interpret New Testament principles without drawing up a church discipline? How can we adjust today's living to Christ's teaching and example? There's no easy solution, but shall we throw up our hands and do nothing? This can't be the answer.

We get these issues from many angles—from teens who want the green light so they can get in on what everyone's doing, from youth who are alarmed over shady trends, from parents and leaders who swing to either one extreme or the other, and from those who are trying to follow the New Testament in the Spirit of Christ.

Thoughtful Christians have no desire to backtrack to ironclad rules, which produce intolerant whims. And yet they are confronted with unmistakable signs of moral decay. Experts in the fields most closely related to juvenile behavior point out serious letdowns in personal standards which were once taken for granted. The church cannot remain silent while the sinister forces boldly undermine the foundations of Christian society. Let no parent say, "There is nothing I can do." You owe it to your children to pass on the solid anchor your own parents gave you.

We need not be apprehensive about setting up standards which will mean sacrifice and hard discipline. Youth are asking for the real Christian pathway through a confused and complex world. We can point the way through sustained home and church cooperation.

Three key words in the Bible verses which follow, express the role of parents and youth leaders—*command, teach, example* (show): "These things command and teach . . . but be thou an example of the believers, in word, in conversation [conduct], in charity, in spirit, in faith, in purity" (1 Tim. 4:11-12). If we can *show* the Christian path in all these areas of day-to-day living, perhaps our youth will be ready to listen to what we command and teach.

But we must remember that it takes time to grow a mature personality; it takes years for an adolescent to grow up. And while he is growing he needs the support, encouragement, and guidance of adults who love and understand. As we listen to what our teens say, shall we consider the specific problems of their day and world? Shall we endeavor to glean from them more effective ways of leading youth to Christ and of helping them grow in Christlike conduct, in faith, and in doctrine? As we listen to the questions teens ask, shall we venture to raise a few guideposts to steer parents and leaders—shepherds of the Way, the Truth and the Life?

To about five hundred college students (representing half the states), I put this question: What was your greatest teen-age problem? They wrote themes for English classes frankly expressing their gripes and airing their problems. Chapter one is a brief review on these themes. The other chapters in the book are based on hundreds of letters written into "Christian Teen Topics," which is a regular feature of *Youth* magazine.

This is my concern and hope: To inspire faith and understanding between adults and youth—to keep before youth the highest goals of the New Testament—to challenge youth to achieve through difficulties the highest excellence within their reach.

CONTENTS

1

> The adolescent, unsure of his own goals, keenly feels the impact of social confusion. Because of his own confusion he seeks an answer outside himself. He tries to find it both in his own family group and in the world outside his family. Neither group can give him rules of living which are without contradiction. He is sharply aware of the confusion in our social structure.*

WHY CALL US DELINQUENT?

Most teen-agers do not get a chance to talk back, but hundreds did—at our request. In themes written for college English, they said something like this: We resent being called delinquent. Are we a lost generation—lawless, sex-mad, shiftless, drunken? Seventeen million of us refute the accusation. Why not give more recognition to the 97 percent of us who are trying to comport ourselves in a manner worthy of your teaching? We face enormous chances of wrecking body and soul—adults provide us smooth lessons by way of movies, television, and cheap literature.

You Say We Are Lawless

Teens answer that only about 3 percent of young people get into serious trouble. And in a study conducted by Harvard University results show that three out of every five juvenile lawbreakers come from homes that are broken or festering discord.

"The families of our grandparents worked, played, and worshiped together," Jerry wrote for English 101. "We do all these things, but we do them separately; each member is independent in his own interests. If family unity were brought back to its former level, I think we would have fewer maladjusted teenagers."

---

*From *The Adolescent and His World,* Irene M. Josselyn, M.D. (copyright 1952 by Family Service Association of America, New York), p. 27. Used by permission of publishers.

"I believe we should look first at the home life," wrote Mac. "I was raised in a pleasant and cheerful atmosphere. There were no parental conflicts, for Mother and Dad showed the highest respect for each other. Love was plentiful, and it has lasted through the years."

In his senior term of high school Mac fell in with a rough crowd, but he said, "That inward desire for a better way of living soon brought me back to my senses."

Ann wrote: "Can you imagine my embarrassment? At high school graduation I had to introduce my four parents—two sets of them—to teachers and classmates."

You Say We Resent Controls

Many students voiced the need for curfews and other controls—as did Bob: "Parents should not slack off on discipline because of physical growth. Maturity of the mind is far behind that of the body. A few restrictions are a must."

Fay expressed the right idea: "I am proud that my parents are interested enough in my well-being to require sensible standards. It gives me a feeling of security and does not make me feel less grown up."

Jack declared that he had fallen into habits of drinking and gambling because of no controls in the home. "When I was out at a bar until 3:00 A.M. Mom and Dad never seemed to care. They didn't ask me where I'd been or what I was doing. No thanks to them that I straightened out."

Betty, who hated the word "curfew," decided to try a little psychology on her mother. She started coming home fifteen minutes earlier than the time her mother set. She says, "It worked. No more curfews for me. Just show your parents that you can take care of yourself. Remember, they are looking out for your good because they love you enough to worry over you."

You Think We Are Sex Crazy

"There were about forty boys and girls in our high school crowd," said Elaine. "At our parties we never allowed drinking or heavy petting. I don't feel that I have missed anything or have been oppressed by the ideals I have held."

Wrote Mike: "When I take my girl out riding I discover that

10

she is warm and full of life. Then comes the problem of petting. Keeping it to a minimum is the only safe way. The majority of fellows wish to steer clear of such emotional tangles."

The unique aspect of modern dating is that moral responsibility rests entirely on teen-agers themselves—the days of chaperones are past. The only protection against sex impulses are moral standards. Here again parents have large responsibility. If a pattern has been set deep within the woof and warp of their being, teens will most likely follow that pattern.

You Say You Can't Understand Us

"The most common complaint of teen-agers against parents is their inability to understand; they do not try to come down on our level to discuss a problem," said Jane, who happily added, "But my Dad is not like that. He says that he has confidence in me, and explains just why I must be careful—like not sitting in a parked car in a remote place to talk."

Another teen wrote: "Older people think they have troubles and woes over such minor things as where the next month's rent is coming from. But they haven't seen problems until they have talked to a teen-ager. Take dating. It's heartbreak, despair, and yet it's heaven!"

Harry, who had been the leader of a wild clan, wrote: "It is only by the grace of God that I escaped the fate of my buddies who served prison terms. So take the advice of one who was a delinquent: The solution would be simple if people would stop threatening and try to see things as youth see them. The differences between my dad and me were discussed only in a family brawl. We never talked things over except in a heated argument."

You Say That We Are Shiftless

"When will you change the antiquated laws which force us youngsters under eighteen into years of idleness? We need play and fun, but even more we need self-respecting jobs that will help us on the road to maturity."

Boys and girls given responsibility in their early teens usually develop qualities of leadership and moral fitness when they leave home to enter college or the armed forces. Said Don: "My dad gave me an allowance and saw that I spent it wisely, but I still feel that I was cheated. Dad boasts of getting up before

11

dawn to feed the animals and milk the cows. What can I tell my sons?"

Ronnie found his job the biggest factor in shaping his personality. "I carried the *Evening Bulletin* for five years," he said. "The weather was never too cold for me to enjoy my paper route. There is no better way to get to know people—how they keep house, how they like the preacher, what they think of the president. I listened to their everyday troubles when they called me in for a hot cup of chocolate. I think that's why it is easy for me to make friends today."

One shy lad wrote: "My confidence rose high when Dad turned over to me the care of all the new calves. I'll always remember those bright spring days after school when I rode my pony over the prairie counting the baby calves."

You Say We Seek Mad Thrills

Are we robbing our children of the simple "familyship" our foreparents enjoyed? The crowded busy kitchen, the big dining table, the basket dinner on the beach, the burnt ashy hot dogs around a fire in the woods, the aroma of sizzling fish frying on the banks of a creek, and the dear happy faces—what else can leave such thrilling memories?

"Where to go, what to do on a date is always a problem," wrote Nan. "If the school or church has no activity planned, we are tempted just to 'park' somewhere. Yet we know this is not a good practice for two people in love. Even a student center, where a couple can relax and talk, is a big asset to a community. When I have a family, I don't want my children walking the streets. I want them to feel free to bring their friends home whenever they please."

The 275,000 teens in YMCA and YWCA societies and the 400,000 members of Boys' Clubs across the nation say that youth prefer clean fun to mad thrills.

You Class Us As Alcoholics

In every instance (according to their essays) the students who favored drinking had parents who sanctioned drinking either by word or practice. The Harvard report shows that six out of every ten juvenile delinquents have fathers who drink to excess. Many have mothers who drink.

Dick said, "Teen-agers who smoke, drink, or gamble are immature and insecure. It is really the fault of American parents; they are the ones who should be fined." And Durward wrote, "Give teens a decent place to hang out and they'll be glad to help stamp out the alcoholic problem."

You Say We Are Reckless Drivers

Sid wrote: "One way to solve this problem: In many cities police give teen-age drivers a place to show off and to let off steam. They put the boys through rigid tests and reward the winners. The local papers give recognition to the club. While learning respect for the police and traffic laws, teen-agers can drive crazy without too great risk to themselves and others. I know because I'm a member of such a club."

Because four out of ten high schools include driver education in their courses, students are learning to drive and survive. They have the advantage of better eyesight and faster reflexes. "If dads will give us the right example in carefulness and courtesy, I think we will follow through.

You Say We Are a Godless Generation

The Harvard studies show that very few delinquents have had religious training of any kind. They are the unfortunates who come from unhappy abnormal homes. But there is widespread interest in religion; many of the students reflected this in their essays.

"What can I put my feet on that is firm enough not to tumble?" Rob earnestly asked. "I need someone who does not think *this* today and *that* tomorrow."

Billy gave an answer: "In our home prayer was as natural as eating—grace at every meal and family worship in the evening. Dad built a small room with a little window to let in the sunlight. There one could be alone with his thoughts and God."

And Jerry added, "More than anything else, family worship smoothed out problems and kept our home united. How could we share in worship of God without forgiving and loving each other?"

A significant minority have flung their bitterness into the face of a society that has denied them love and control in their formative years. But many implore the pulpit and press, air and screen to let up on teen-age crime publicity. "Give us a chance to do as well as you have done."

1. How can parents and other leaders offset the "impact of social confusion"?

2. Think of ways to give recognition to worthy young people.

3. How can you *encourage* teens at home? At church?

4. How can we provide acceptable guidance?

5. Have we tried listening?

6. What about jobs for teens?

7. Describe the climate of an ideal home.

8. What controls are a must?

9. Consider: The importance of harmony between ideals and practice.

10. Are you giving your teens an anchor which will hold?

2

Mutual dependency is a universal characteristic
of the human race.*

CAN'T THEY SEE I'M GROWING UP?

Your Teens Say

"Recently a boy asked me to go to a party, but my parents say I'm too young to date. Often I try to talk to my mother and tell her how I feel, but she ignores me. What can a girl of fifteen do to make her mother understand?"

"I am a boy of seventeen and love a girl almost fifteen. Since her parents won't let her date, she slips around and comes to my house, but my mother does not like this. All we want is a chance to prove that we are old enough to know how to act on a date."

"What can I do or say to make my father let me go out on dates? I'm almost sixteen, and Mother would let me go to football games, but Dad says I only go to hang out with boys. He acts as if he has no confidence in me and makes me feel like a hypocrite. I've thought of running away, but that wouldn't be right. Why can't he see that I'm growing up?"

Early Dating

A girl of only twelve wrote about being in love with a boy and his uncle. Both are "living dolls," she reported. The girls around fourteen all say, "I look much older." How can parents cope with this universal fad of early dating?

Instead of a flat refusal, why not clearly state your reasons and give teens a chance to express their feelings on the subject? In this way you can hope to retain their confidence, even when the final answer is No. If you decide against regular dating for the early teens, then you need to provide alternatives.

Parents might as well face the issue squarely: These teens need parents—need their time, their understanding, their concern, their affection, their money, and their sharpest planning. The predating years must be filled with wholesome opportunities for mingling of boys and girls in happy and safe situations.

---

*From *The Adolescent and His World*, Josselyn, p. 49.

Of course, having frequent open-house sessions for teens and their friends means that Mom and Dad will have little time for a social life of their own. However, there are compensations, for there's never a dull hour around these lively youngsters. In later years when problems are forgotten, parents will look back with nostalgia and wish for the happy noise of former days.

Not many admit it, but don't we all feel at times like a mother who recently sighed, "I'll be glad when my girls grow up and have homes of their own"? This mother frankly admitted that she did not know how to manage her teens, who were getting rather out-of-hand. But all parents can learn, if they persistently seek for the helps they need. We can't afford to throw off the greatest opportunity of our lives.

Parents, of course, represent the church as well as the home. There is fellowship in sharing common problems, and in sharing work and responsibilities in the recreational program of the church.

When we consider the fruits of too early pairing off, we cannot but take a dim view of the practice. Look at the increase in teen-age marriages and subsequent divorce, the number of illegitimate babies, and the shocking report of venereal diseases among teens. Later on we shall discuss the pros and cons of going steady, but for now the question is: What can parents do when "mere children" want to date?

First of all, prepare yourself and your children for the romantic years just around the corner. One set of parents, looking several years ahead, provided books for adolescents (and I'm sure Mom and Dad read them first). One mother obtained for her son and daughter books inscribed with their names. Inside she wrote, "To be read when you are twelve." The books spelled security to these children who lost their mother one month before the girl reached twelve. Your church publishing house can supply you with books which will help you and your growing teens.

Before they begin to date, teach your girls and boys the principles which you hope will be their guiding stars through the perilous years ahead. Long before the dating urge brings its problems, fortify them with deeply embedded Christian ideals translated into down-to-earth examples.

Do not abdicate authority. The adolescent may resent it now, but in a few years he will thank you. If, on the other hand, as an irresponsible parent, you hand over the reins and let him do the driving, he will surely harbor resentments against you the rest of his life. Perhaps you as a parent or church leader are terribly uncertain about all the questions your junior highs and older teens are asking. Maybe you have not settled in your own mind the basic ethics of Christian belief and conduct. Then it is high time that through prayer, consecration, and study, you set your own life purposes and goals.

Mom and Dad must agree on controls and policies in the home —this is imperative. All major differences should·be thrashed out in private so that the two may stand together in the point of view decided upon.

I clearly remember the closed-door conferences of my father and mother—though to this day I remain in the dark as to what they were about. It seemed natural to us children that parents discuss problems, and we knew that what either said was law and gospel with the other. If they had bitter disagreements, we never knew it. Incidentally, they must have discussed a great many things we never heard about, such as church differences and sins and faults of members. As far as we knew, our church leaders of those days were one and all hallowed saints. It didn't hurt us, either, to be late in discovering the fallibility of people. At least the pattern was etched: to trust every one until he proved untrustworthy, instead of vice versa. When parents agree, the battle is half won.

We never outgrow authority, nor do we wish to. But we would be quick to resent unjust and selfish rule. So with parents it isn't the strictness or firmness that provoke boys and girls to run away from home—at least want to run away—it's the way parents go about making and enforcing home-rule. Many fathers lack courage to utter a firm command or refusal unless they lose their temper and speak in anger. But the parent who resorts to loud and angry demonstrations exposes his own weaknesses and thereby suffers loss of respect. A serene but firm manner is always more effective.

For many sincere parents the rule is: Never correct a child in anger. A period of waiting gives time for prayerful evaluation, and when it becomes necessary to lay down an ultimatum, you will not likely regret it.

Are They Ready for Dating?

How can a mother and dad know when their Sonny or Sue should start dating? Should this important decision be left entirely up to the young person? What is the proper criterion? A certain age? Social pressures? Desire to be grown up? The biological urge?

A poll was taken of one thousand high school students who were asked the question of when teens should start dating. The students' answers ranged from age thirteen to age sixteen. The poll revealed that 31 percent actually dated before they were fourteen. This is not surprising in view of prevailing customs—romantic mothers hustle their little girls, still in grammar school, into grown-up attire such as sophisticated dresses. Paired with unwilling little boys, these children are pushed into premature roles of aping young adults.

But the strongest social pressures come from the adolescent's own peers, where conformity to the age group is of the utmost importance. This spells opportunity for the church. Parents may band together, agree on rules of behavior, and provide a program of well-supervised activities which meet the needs for social intermingling of the sexes.

Often the girls and boys who verbalize an interest in each other are only playing a game. They are not emotionally ready for a genuine interest in members of the other sex, but they do want to produce evidence of growing up, of leaving behind patterns of childhood.

Variation in rate of maturing presents special problems to both the adolescent and his parents. If maturation is slower than the average rate, the girl or boy out of step with his age group may find anxieties quite overpowering. His parents and friends make him feel queer, inadequate, abnormal. On the other hand, if the individual matures early, he is isolated from his chronological age group and excluded from the older set as well.

"The fellow or girl ready to date is one who: knows the facts of life, has proved his or her dependability, knows the courtesies of dating, has adopted a standard of personal conduct."*

In the next chapter we will think together about the role of adults in preparing youth for the years of dating experience.

*Your Dating Data, Verna Joiner (Chapter 1)

Just now, ask yourself: What about the young people in my home, in my church school class, in my youth group? How do they rate in this readiness test? Is their knowledge and view of sex the Hollywood version? Who told them the physical and emotional facts about sex? Who taught them by precept and example the courtesies they need in all interpersonal relationships? Have they adopted a Christian standard of personal conduct?

Have these tween-agers or early teens been given opportunity to develop dependability? Have you as parents carefully increased responsibilities geared to their rate of maturation?

The adolescent is faced with two conflicting needs: the desire and need for independence and the continued need for dependence. Past experience has not prepared him to try out his own resources confidently; and when he does accept a measure of independence, he finds that he still desires to be protected. With human beings, unlike many lower animals, dependency is not abandoned at maturity; the nature of dependency is only modified.

Modern dating customs afford and demand a large degree of freedom. The young couple walk out into the night alone or drive away in a thirdhand jalopy, with no restraints other than their own sense of moral rightness. Have they earned this freedom by proving that they can be trusted out of sight? Have they learned to stand on their own two feet, regardless of what others do or say?

If they have handled their allowances and earnings, accepted their share of home duties, and shared in family planning councils—perhaps they can also handle a bit more independence along social lines. When the inevitable question, Why can't I date? is fired at you, what will be your answer?

SUMMING UP

How can parents and youth leaders cope with the fad of early dating?

Consider the results of too early pairing off.

Prepare yourself.

Prepare youth in your charge.

How important is harmony between parents?

How important is agreement of church leaders on general standards?

What is your criteria for dating readiness?

How can adults satisfy the conflicting needs in their teens, as to independence and dependence?

How can the church train youth in dependability?

Is this your definition of *maturity?*

Responsibility instead of dependence?

Cooperativeness instead of competitiveness?

A *giving* rather than a receiving attitude?

Gentleness, kindness and *goodwill* instead of hostile feelings?

Adaptability instead of stubbornness?

Just how mature are you?

3

Human nature is so thoroughly malleable that it can be shaped to almost any form the culture decrees . . . the home and the family are the basic cultural unit, the major agency through which a culture makes its impact upon the . . . child.*

THEY EXPECT ME TO KNOW

They Expect Me to Know About Sex

"You silly girl!" a mother shamed her twelve-year-old Fayla. The two had watched a small brood of chickens gobble up their feeding of table scraps and corn, when Fayla cried out "Mother, make the rooster stop fighting that hen."

"You silly girl" was the sum of the mother's response.

And that was the first inkling ever to bewilder Fayla's mind as to where chicks and all the other babies came from. With curiosity aroused, she questioned her mother who, greatly embarrassed, confused her daughter still more with incoherent warnings. "Never let a boy kiss you, Fayla, for if you start such things, the next thing you know you may be having a baby."

Instantly Fayla recalled the party at a friend's house—Denny had kissed her! Would she be disgraced by having a baby? For two years she struggled with this problem, not daring to tell anyone her fears.

Extreme case? The abundance of sex-centered films and other media lead us to think so; but some of the letters, hesitantly expressed, cause me to wonder.

"I have started going steady," writes a young girl, "How can I keep from getting pregnant?"

In a recent letter a girl is extremely upset because friends have been talking "sex" in her presence. She says, "I know nothing at all about sex and I don't want to know—please tell me some things." And in the next sentence: "Forget about my

*From *The Psychology of Adolescent Development*, Raymond G. Kuhlen. Used by permission of Harper & Row.

questions; I'm so ashamed for asking you—don't write me, don't even pray for me—I'll never mention it again."

We dare not assume that teens are safe in simply knowing the physical facts of life; they may be sadly ignorant of the emotional implications of sex. We do know that most young people only dimly realize the dynamic force of their sexual feelings. "Sex has been called the most powerful force in the world."

Boys need to understand how to avoid situations that lead to loss of controls. Girls need to know what boys are made of —how they differ emotionally from their sisters.

The Christian point of view must be made unmistakably clear: premarital intercourse is wrong. The old triple fears are ever present: "Fear of infection, conception, and detection." But even though a pair escape all three threats, multiple records prove results full of disappointment, guilt, and poor marriage adjustment. The deep pools of doubt, hypocrisy, and distrust are difficult to redeem. People who break the "law of love" disrupt their own self-esteem.

Parents cannot always "police" their inexperienced boys and girls. Their only safety lies in moral values taught through patient understanding, just discipline, and Christlike example.

They Expect Me to Know the Rules

Take nothing for granted. It is dangerous to *assume* that Bobby knows the speed limits when you warn, "Don't drive too fast." Make sure that he knows *your* limits, plus traffic regulations. Likewise, be dead certain that Susie understands the meaning of "Don't go too far!" How far is too far when a young couple are alone and in love?

Mrs. Lawrence S. Rockefeller as chairman of World Service Council of YWCA of U.S.A. said in a "Journal Forum" that in all areas of right and wrong, "the home is the hub; churches, schools and other community agencies help." She points out that young people to a great extent follow the example of their parents. "If parents are dishonest, if they cheat, children are likely to do the same."

Another participant in that forum, Robert E. Fitch, said, "People are less certain today than they have been at some times in the past what the basic moral values are." And Adlai Stevenson asked the forum, "Has indignation become unfashionable?" Later he lamented the trend to sidestep moral ethics and virtues by mumbling, "Who am I to say what is right or wrong?" or "Whatever you can get away with is permissible."

Teen-agers grow up to appreciate the disciplines exercised in their homes; they honor parents who have the wisdom to set limits and enforce them. The frequent letters from teens who threaten to run away from home, describe fathers and mothers who "don't understand—don't trust me—won't listen." The most hopeless cry of all: "I can't talk to my parents."

Keep the line of communication in working order—remember it is two-way: listening and talking. You don't know what to say until you *listen,* until you discover the real problem behind words and actions. Not that you always agree—teens don't expect you to sanction all they say. After all, they don't mean half the things they vehemently voice; they are reaching out for something solid amidst conflicting ideas. To ridicule and deny, to ignore and rebuff, to shut them up when they express popular opinions—these are sure ways to block further communication. No need to be shocked; often they don't believe it either. But they want to hear positive affirmations based on sound logic, logic which has been tested and confirmed through personal application. Oh, they may do a bit of testing themselves, but they will adopt, though reluctantly, the moral standard which you have consistently taught and practiced.

Parents not only *can,* they *do* shape the character of the young lives entrusted to them, for home is the first and most important of all cultural agencies.

They Expect Me to Know Etiquette

Basically, practice of the Golden Rule underwrites the manners of refined family living. Through kindly concern of other's welfare, members learn the courtesies which will carry over into social life outside the home. Dad exhibits tender respect as he seats Mother before he takes his place at the head of the table. Mother sees that Dad gets his easy chair when he comes home tired in the evening. Such attitudes in thoughtfulness are easily caught by young observers. Mothers especially need to take time in the very middle of the rush to teach proper table manners. And Dad, of course, requires a reverent pause before offering thanks at meals.

I know a young woman who values her precious china and

23

crystal above all other material possessions, but she takes special delight in setting a lovely table and serving her best dinner for her own family. Can you picture the children from this home in later polite society? They should be able to handle the common courtesies, not merely from the books, but from everyday practice.

Before teens begin dating they should feel secure about dating etiquette. Unless *he* has been taught, how is a boy to know that it is manly, not sissy, to open the door for a girl, to help her with her wrap, to hold her chair at the table? How can a girl know her role in dating customs unless she has been taught? Of course, both learn quickly enough the popular version of how to act on a date. But only the young people with special Christian training know for themselves the proper and right choice in each situation.

Your Teens Want to Know

"Is it all right for a boy of fourteen to go with a girl the same age when her parents take them in their car? When we go to a school game, I pay for the girl, but not for the parents. Should I? I could hardly afford it."

—Boy from Kansas

"Is it true or not that you have to be in love with a girl to date her? Could you give me some tips on asking a girl for a date?"

—Boy from Oklahoma

"I've gone with several girls, but when I ask for a second date, they always turn me down. Is this because I am too shy to kiss a girl?"

—Boy from California

"I have a question I wish you would answer quick. How do you tell a boy you like him and think he is pretty wonderful? I asked my parents but they do not know."

—Girl from Oregon

"I like a boy who does not seem to know that I exist. Is it ever proper for a girl to invite a boy to her house or to a special church activity?"

—Girl from Ohio

24

When the home library includes at least one good book on etiquette, every member of the family finds numerous occasions to refer to the book. The company is sending Dad to a convention—what should he know about tipping? Mom is invited to a banquet—what shall she wear? Is she sure of correct procedure at the table?

Teens look up all sorts of questions. What's what in various sports? How make introductions? What rules apply to letter writing? How make a guest feel at home? And when there's a wedding coming up, the etiquette book is constantly in use.

Perhaps there are parents who will say that these things are not important—good morals and spiritual welfare certainly take priority over social etiquette. But when you visit that son or daughter away at college (or elsewhere), you would like for your child to feel that his parents know the proper thing to do and say. Even though you have had little time or opportunity to brush up on social graces, anyone can learn basic principles of polite manners. It's never too late to learn, but it can be too late to instill good habits in your children.

Parents who expect their boys and girls to know the physical and emotional facts of life—safe moral standards and proper social manners—will find ways for growing with their teens. Through research, study, prayer, deep thinking, and conferring with other concerned adults, you can together set your goals and aims for family living. You need to think through a great many questions, old familiar problems but in new settings and with new implications. "I do not want my child to think of me as a *know-it-all* but always as a *learner*," says one mother.

"Every learner has a goal or purpose," writes Ronald C. Doll. "It involves value clarification, attitude formation and change, structuring, acquisition of skills, implanting of new appreciations."

Summing Up

1. Do you expect your teens to know about:

   Emotional involvements of sex?
   The Christian view on sex?
   The Christian standard of conduct?
   Proper social manners?

2. What are your methods for getting this information to them?

3. How can home and church work together in training teens for dating?

4. What avenues of learning are available to busy adults?

5. Has the general moral slump affected the standards of your local youth group?

6. What can you do as a parent or leader of youth to lift the spiritual and moral sights of your church?

4

The importance of the home in the formation of religious beliefs is indicated by the fact that in an extensive survey of young people in Maryland, it was found that 81 percent of those with some religious affiliation had adopted the faith of their parents.*

CONFUSED ABOUT BEING A CHRISTIAN

If my teen letters are a true indication, then nothing in all the world is more important to the younger generation than the assurance of salvation. Surprised? Let us thank God and take courage.

Your Teens Say

"I am a fourteen-year-old boy. A couple of years ago I was saved in the parsonage of our church. After a while I backslid, then later was saved again and baptized. But after I was saved the second time, I fussed with my classmates and family, and I let up on prayer and reading my Bible. Now I have started living closer to God, but I want to know if I should repent and be saved all over again. I am asking forgiveness for my wrong-doings *then* and *now*, but I am still in doubt about being a Christian. Please pray for me and help me, for you can see that my problems are strange and serious . . ."

—Boy from West Virginia

"I am only twelve years old, and I would like to know if it would look silly for me to go to the altar. I want to go so badly; it would make me happy to give my life to Christ, but only adults go to the altar in our church. I'm almost sure that I would feel out of place. I would really appreciate it if you would tell me what to do."

—Girl from Indiana

---

*Kuhlen, p. 445.

"I would like so much to get my life all in line with God. I have gone to church all my life but still am not a Christian. I am so mixed up I don't know what to do. Please advise me and pray for me.

—Girl from Oklahoma

"I have been saved twice, but I feel that the Lord is not with me. What can I do to increase my faith and to restore my folks' faith in me?"

—Girl from the South

"I want to give my whole heart to God, but I just can't do it. Maybe you should just give me up and stop praying for me."

—Girl from Arizona

Make It Simple

Parents! Pastors! Evangelists! Teachers! Are you sure that you are making the way of salvation plain? So simple that even a child can follow through? All too often a young "seeker" does not receive at the altar the instructions and definite help he needs. Perhaps the altar worker assumes that the youth is already a Christian. One should tactfully ask, "What is your need?" We should encourage a definite commitment and act of faith. This should be a crisis experience, followed by baptism (for a new convert) and active fellowship in the group.

Who is to shepherd these young sheep, so often losing their way after Christ has saved them? Do we stand back and measure them by adult standards? Think, think back. How often were you frustrated as a teen-age Christian? How many times did you promise God: "I *will* live closer to you. I will pray more. I won't talk back to my mother. I won't quarrel with my brother or sister"? And how many times did you fail and God forgive? Seventy times seven?

The most important thing on earth for a young Christian to know is what to do when he fails. Teach him to make things right immediately. Explain to him what John said: "My little children, these things write I unto you, that ye sin not. And if any man sin, we have an advocate with the Father, Jesus Christ the righteous" (1 John 2:1). Teach them by your own example. Humbly admit your own mistakes and ask forgiveness. Your young people will respect and admire you for it. Are you close enough to your teens to talk over experiences? Something like this:

"I don't feel that I'm a very good Christian," a lad said to his mother after listening to a searching message Sunday morning. "If I can't do better than this, sometimes I think I might as well give up trying. Or maybe I should start all over again. Should I?"

"Son, I've often felt the same way," the mother answered, "especially when I was much younger. I was terribly full of doubts."

"You, Mom, you felt like that?"

"Yes, Sonny, I've had to struggle to overcome so many faults —often felt discouraged. But suppose I had given up? That would never do. And don't think that I've arrived—the goal is still far ahead. It will always be. Don't you see, that's what keeps Christian living so exciting."

"I think I see," Sonny agreed, "but I never dreamed that it was like that with you, Mom. You've always been so—so good."

"I'm proud to see you reaching higher, Son. Makes me know you're a growing Christian. I'm glad you went up to the altar to pray this morning. You may feel a need to go many, many times to ask for strength and guidance, and even forgiveness— but that does not mean you've lost out with God. It means that you are determined to measure up to the light God gives you. Just as you are growing physically, you are also growing to be a more mature Christian, with God's help."

"Thanks, Mom, thanks a lot."

Make It Attractive

When ideals (or doctrines) integrate into happy religious experiences, they become a dynamic part of one's personality. Men do not make religion attractive when they present it as a soft, spineless way of life. The Christ who said, "Follow me," also said, "Take up thy cross." Lift up Christ; he is the drawing power of Christianity.

Dr. Charles Malik, former president of the U.N., was asked where Christianity has failed in opposing communism. He replied that there is too much "softheadedness—I could recite twenty or more signs of moral weakness—Christians aren't speaking with conviction—many Christians have become worldly . . ."

Many things under the name of religion repel youth. Narrow, dogmatic preaching repels. Quibbling over nonessentials repels. Watered-down doctrine repels. A cold, lifeless church holds no attraction for the young seeker of the Way, the Truth, and the Life.

The Christ and Christ-way of the New Testament appeals to youth searching for a cause great enough to demand life-devotion. Living men and women facing adversity courageously—missionaries, nurses, and doctors pouring out their life blood for God. These appeal most strongly to youth. But so also do the local men and women who live Christ joyously and lovingly in the office, the shop, the schoolroom, the home, and the church.

Make It Important

At church we may sing, "Lord, take the first place in my heart," and, "I surrender all." But in the day-to-day happenings does he occupy first position? Or do cares of life and cravings to possess material comforts push back spiritual impulses?

One girl wrote something like this: "My Dad is a walking Bible, thinks he knows all there is to know about religion; but he doesn't live it at home. He never has a kind word for Mother and won't listen to anything we say."

"Peace be to this house!" So gave the disciples their benediction upon the homes which received them. And God's peace does still abide and bless where Christ abides. Christ controls the "wild horses" of emotions and nerves, calms anxieties, supplies strength for the day and grace for the moment. He offers faith, hope, and love which never run out.

The externals of religion are important only when they spring from right motives. Church attendance, tithes and offerings, testimonies, even defense of the Bible, these may all be lifeless forms which hold no charm. The Spirit of Christ is humble, loving, forgiving.

While the large majority of children adopt the faith of their parents, what of the smaller percentage who pull up roots and turn to other creeds? Are they looking for a religion vital enough to change lives? To produce fruits of integrity, kindness, courage, and trust? In your church, and in your home, what are the things of first importance?

Make It Personal

In your church school, in your class, in your youth group, in your family, there are young people ready for a crucial encounter with Christ. In spite of various experiences at church, they are still confused about being a Christian. They doubt that anything real has happened within. At least they are troubled and vaguely uncertain about the whole matter.

Of course, the Holy Spirit works personally with each individual, and he reaches many through general evangelistic efforts. But how much more effectual can the Holy Spirit work with a person through another person. This is the great need—Spirit led persons to lead the individual boy or girl to a personal experience with Christ.

The young man who said, "You can see that my problems are strange and serious"—his needs were distinctly personal, though common to so many other teens. Whether or not he had experienced the new birth in the past, that question need not continue to frustrate and hold him back. Now, at this moment, he can in an instant of faith accept full pardon for past mistakes and sins. He can take it from this point and go on from grace to growth in Christ. That is, he can do this with continued encouragement and personal counsel.

Over and over the same young people seek spiritual help. We surely would not want to discourage their efforts. But are we really helping them to make progress? Are we teaching them to put into practice the disciplines which will mean growth toward spiritual maturity? Are we leading them to put into action their good resolves? Because if we are not, the results may be disastrous. Our golden opportunity passes, and with it the hope of enlisting these young lives for Christian service.

Was it a pastor who said to his own teen-age boy, "If I couldn't be a better example than that, I'd quit professing"? Sure, the minister was under pressure from some of his members. Their children had exerted a bad influence over the "preacher's kid." But you know who gets all the blame. Still, the pastor has a responsibility to his own house; his son is important too. A wise preacher taught: "A bruised reed shall he not break, and the smoking flax shall he not quench" (Isa. 42:3). Reproof, correction, restraint—these are necessary too. Yet, they are effective only when administered in love. Never discourage a young

Christian however weak and immature he seems. He needs help.

Make It Workable

Teens want more than high-sounding ideologies. We must recapture the Master's methods of plain teaching in terms related to everyday living. We must teach what sin *is* and what it is *not*—how to distinguish between right and wrong, and better and the best. Messages of hope and daring motivate more effectually than repeated warnings of doom. Teens want and desperately need a religion that will enable them to cope with the difficulties and opportunities they now face. They need a way of life, but more, they need a Way, a Person. In Christ they will discover both an adequate theology and a Friend and Sustainer.

Move over and make room for young inexperienced workers. Every new Christian should fall heir to a place to serve in the program of the church. Be the task ever so small, make it significant; let him know that the church needs him now to serve and to prepare for the future. Teach youth to witness. The boy or girl who stands in a youth service or prayer meeting and testifies to Christ's saving grace—this young Christian will sense a greater responsibility to live his religion. He will develop courage to stand up for his convictions in school and social life. Nothing puts life into a meeting like the burning testimony or prayer of a vibrant youth bursting with life and energy, and ready to set the world on fire. Adults need youth. Let us not relegate all their activities to Youth Fellowship.

In the home, too, young people can share in planning and leading worship. They may help younger brothers or sisters prepare a church school lesson, or they may tell or read Bible stories to the younger ones.

Teens enjoy helping a sick neighbor, caring for a child, cooking a meal, reading to a blind person. These acts of kindness take on deeper meaning when they are done in the name of Christ as a vital part of Christian living—not just as a duty, but as love in action. Bubbling over with pep and punch, these teens want a hearty religion filled with activity—work as well as fun. Not just *to be* Christian, but to be *doing* from morning till night—that's your teens.

Religion must be more than a study of Bible persons, places, doctrines, and rules. Teen Christians must test out and apply theology to every situation—to every problem they meet. For them religion must work.

Make It Prayerful

To be powerful, religion must be prayerful. Teens need power at their fingertips for instant help in temptation, for courage to stand by convictions, for know-how to perform a difficult task. Adults must support young people in their dependency needs and also their needs for limited independence. Do we encourage teens to share their problems with us, that we may counsel and pray with them? Are we teaching them to pray? They too must know the joy of communing with God, the comfort of his assuring Presence, the guidance of his Holy Spirit.

More time given over to participation in silent group praying may be one means of learning to pray. Prayer should precede and follow every Christian act, for prayer is Christian action. Let us teach youth to avail themselves of this greatest source of help. We may assist them through helpful literature, through quiet times with them, through sharing our own deeper experiences. Our own praying will impress teens to the extent that it spills over and saturates our thinking, talking, and acting. Let *us* pray.

SUMMING UP

1. Make it simple, lucid, clear!
2. Make it attractive!
3. Make it important, challenging!
4. Make it personal!
5. Make it practical, workable, vital!
6. Make it prayerful!

5

One of the safeguards of the teen-age group is the fact that individuals in that rank are strict conformists. Often this fact is overlooked because the conformity is not to the standards of the home. The conformity is to the standards of the peer group. What the group approves is right. What it disapproves is wrong. . . . If the group is a desirable one, there is no need for concern. If it is an undesirable group, one faces a strong antagonist.*

NOWHERE TO GO ON A DATE

Your Teens Say

"I am fourteen, but people say I act and look much older. I would like to go out double dating and riding around Sunday afternoons two or three hours. My mother won't let me go out much because she says I'm too young. Do you agree with my mother? She is very nice though; she lets my boyfriend come to my house and we cook and eat pizzas, but even this gets boring. What can we do?"

—Girl from Ohio

"I am fifteen and have a big problem. What should I say to a boy if he asks me out to someplace I feel I shouldn't go? How can I make him understand? I don't want him to think that I am a creep. Even my best girl friend calls me queer for not going to different places with her. When they call me names I just laugh at them, but I really feel like telling them off. Should I just keep laughing?"

—Girl from the North

"I am old enough to date, but my parents will hardly let me out of their sight. My dad tags along with me—treats me like a child. Where can I take a girl under such circumstances? Do you think I should leave home? I can't put up with this much longer."

—Boy from Ohio

*From *Psychosocial Development of Children,* Irene M. Josselyn, M.D., pp. 108-109. Copyright, 1948, by Family Association of America, New York.

"Where can I take a girl on dates? How often should we date? How late should we stay out? And should I kiss her good-night?"

—Boy from Pennsylvania

"I don't want to do anything that is wrong, but there never seems to be anything for us Christian teen-agers to do in the way of having fun without someone saying we're doing wrong— whether we go to shows, roller skating, or bowling. What activities can we take part in? Where can a Christian girl and boy go on a date and no one point a finger?"

—Girl from Kentucky

"In our city we have a youth center where young people can meet and play table tennis, dance, or listen to rock'n'roll. We have our parents as counselors and there are strict rules to obey."

—Girl from Oklahoma

Are your teens driving over lonely roads or hunting distant places of amusement because there seems to be nothing else to do? Do they park and sit and talk because there is no proper nook to carry on a conversation without family at their elbows? When the sports season is over at school, where can Bill take Sue on their weekly Friday night date?

What *can* the fifteen-year-old tell her friends, both boys and girls, who ask her to go places which are off limits because of her own standards or those of her church or her parents? Can she proudly present counter plans? What are the alternatives? Are you one quick to point a finger, to criticize, yet slow to lift a finger to help? Just what are your restrictions about social entertainment, places of amusement, where not to go and what not to do? Are your rules understood? In other words, do you make it clear *why* you (or your church) object to certain popular activities? Do you yourself know the answer?

In some communities, concerned parents, teachers, and other school and church leaders, get together to discuss these problems. They arrive at a few conclusions about places of entertainment and time to be home. Then they call a meeting which includes the young people. There they put the plan before them and give them opportunity for full expression of their opinions. Often a young group will come up with a more rigid code of regulations than adults would dare to offer. And since teen-agers are such strict conformists to whatever their group sanc-

35

tions, there is little trouble about getting the code established in teen society

But there are still the conflicting standards of various churches—even differences among congregations of the same faith. However, the more Bible-centered and spiritual groups of a community tend to hold similar ideas in regard to social practices. And it is imperative that all real Christians stand together against the tides of worldliness that always have threatened and always will threaten the church.

No one should surrender basic personal ethics in order to co-operate with a community or group project. In isolated instances a Christian family must stand alone. But most often a community group can agree upon broad principles that concern age to begin dating, curfews, dates on school nights, places where liquor is served, et cetera. If your church group can collaborate with other churches of similar beliefs in working out an acceptable code, young dating problems will be less serious. Here follows a suggestive list of questions you might use as a starting point.

1. At what age should dating begin?
2. When are chaperones a must?
3. What curfews? What exceptions?
4. What about functions where beer is served? School banquets meeting at night clubs, et cetera?
5. What rules about smoking?
6. What about going steady?
7. Dates on school nights?
8. What forms of amusement in the community are off bounds?
9. What about petting?
10. Any rules for governing dress?
11. What about allowances?
12. What rules about a couple going alone in an automobile?
13. What about sitting in parked cars?
14. How can teens show disapproval of undesirable behavior?

Where Can We Go?

Having decided on a code of conduct, you still must provide a positive answer to the question: Where can we go and what can we do on dates? In another chapter we shall consider why certain amusements are labeled right or wrong. Right now let us explore ways and means of providing safe and adequate social experiences for our Christian youth. A prerequisite is, of course, Christian fellows and girls.

Now that we have a bunch of eager teens, where shall we find consecrated adults to give their love, their time, and energy? The demand is varied enough to include just about everybody: teachers, counselors, program builders, directors, hostesses, cooks, musicians, band director, craftsmen, Boy Scout and Girl Scout leaders, camping specialists, play directors, and patient, understanding *listeners*.

There should be a coordinating council composed of all the officers from the different youth groups (morning and evening sessions) and the adult leaders—advisers, directors, teachers, and pastor. At a special planning meeting (perhaps a retreat), the entire Youth Fellowship year is roughly outlined: the week-to-week study outlines, the major activities (work projects, camps, retreats, conventions), social get-togethers, and the whole area of recreation as connected with the church.

No church is too poor to provide supervised recreation for its youth. The place of meeting may be a barn, a garage, a park, or a youth center. Community facilities may be used when these public halls are not dominated by a rough crowd. In some cities Christians find bowling alleys and skating rinks suitable places for clean, healthful activity. Pastors and youth leaders organize regular bowling clubs for their teens and young adults.

Open house solves the problem for many alert parents. While all too many mothers and fathers are far too busy building up material comforts or finding social satisfaction for themselves, far too busy to give a party for seniors or go on a picnic with the junior highs, there are other parents who care. There are those who feel that the best years of their lives, from twenty to fifty, belong *with* their children. Many older adults, looking back, would give anything to relive the character-building years, to bring back the ringing laughter and noisy chatter of happy teens.

"Mother, may we help with the progressive party?" asks an excited junior high.

Mother hastily brushes away a frown. She had planned a shopping spree for that afternoon, but that can wait. "Sure, we'll serve the main course," she beams at her daughter, "that is if I can count on your help."

It's work, but then again, it's fun to entertain at home,

whether for a half-dozen friends or open house to the whole group. Mom can enlist the entire family, with a bit of planning. It's easier if you have a rec room, but if not, the location may be the living room; it could be a double garage, or in the summertime, a big backyard. Young people are not particular about the setting—all they need is food and pop and good clean fun.

More often than not, open house may be run on a cooperative plan—boys bring a carton of soft drinks, each girl a plate of snacks. The house may furnish extras, like a couple bowls of dips and potato chips. Open house may tie in with some special day or season, or with a special event. Or it may be a going-away party for a fellow leaving for college or service.

Make It a Work Party

You may hold open house for a planning session of the youth council. Or the entire group may be welcomed to a poster contest, posters being made to publicize some special rally or project. Or it could be a rehearsal party, when the group have been working hard on producing a play. Then again, the excuse may be making decorations for the Sweetheart Banquet near Valentine Day. Or a more serious purpose—planning a visitation program before youth revival.

Always, parents must be on hand at these parties, though not necessarily every minute in sight. They need not hesitate to ask troublemakers to behave or leave. The group soon learns the rules of the house, for every Christian home should have a few clearly defined rules. No drinking, of course. No smoking either, no obscene language, no pairing off in dark or out-of-the-way places. Time for breaking up is clearly announced beforehand—and strictly adhered to. This is necessary if parties are to be frequent, work and school considered.

Encourage Hobbies

Music offers variety for a family or for youth who love to play some instrument, sing, or just listen. Why not start a small orchestra or choral club? Songfests can be great joy; there are many favorites which never grow old. Reserve sacred music for the worshipful atmosphere which is usually planned to come near the close of the party or club meeting. You could work up to it with a few spirituals. Your friendship circle easily can turn into a prayer circle as young Christians soberly clasp hands, sing a hymn, and end the evening with prayer. This is a fitting conclusion to any Christian sociality.

Other hobbies or clubs might include: Hi-fi, camera, drama, art, Bible study, science. Girls and fellows who share similar interests should make congenial dating friends. There is room for expanding cultural aptitudes and enjoyments while cultivating worthwhile friends.

Thank God for adults who care enough to give their best in ability, time, and energy, working to build up a real Christian youth group. Since the teens are such strict conformists, one of our greatest problems is that of putting across ·in an acceptable way the basic teachings of the New Testament. For instance, the "group conscience" frowns upon drinking and gambling; therefore, the group standard is accepted and upheld. There will still be numerous opportunities for personal discipline when the young Christian must stand alone in his choice of right against wrong. But spiritual fellowship is as vital to youth as to age. And parents find their own role of training, guiding, and building far more relaxing when they feel comfortable about the teen group.

Summing Up

Do you *point* or *lift* a finger?
Who should decide *where* teens go?
What qualifications are necessary?
Do conflicting standards confuse you, too?
Try making a code of conduct.
What can *you* do to help entertain youth?
Will you give one special ability to the youth of your church?

> Two major temptations confront each generation . . . (1) to accommodate the gospel to the spirit of the age so that there will be no friction between Christians and the world, (2) egotism and pride in moral superiority. . . . The Holy Spirit sanctions neither way.—George Santayna, Spanish philosopher

6

IS THIS WRONG? WHY?

Your Teens Say

"Many of my Christian friends go to the shows, and a lot of them say it's sinful. I go to shows myself, but I'm careful to pick nice, clean, decent shows. What do you think about it?"

—Girl from Kentucky

"What's wrong with dancing if you just dance—not drink, nor let it go any farther? I hope you understand what I mean. I want to become a better Christian. I go to church and pray every night, but something is wrong." —Girl from Indiana

"I am writing about a problem that is bothering a lot of Christian kids. In many churches they never make it clear if it is wrong to go to dances and shows. Still, those who do go are criticized so much that they get discouraged and give up trying to live for Christ." —Girl from Oregon

Young people have a right to know why older Christians label certain amusements as sinful. Children may accept the verdict of parents about what is harmful and what is not, but teens have developed reasoning powers they are eager to test out. They question, argue, and debate until they arrive at an answer which their judgment can accept. It is essential, therefore, that parents and church leaders understand the characteristics of teens and assist them in their search for a workable Christianity.

It is far more important to teach youth the basic principles of the New Testament than to bind upon them a rigid set of rules. Whether we like it or not—God has left a host of choices to the individual conscience. Do we want a cut-and-dried code that requires no personal decision? Such a creed would be as intolerable as the Law of Moses. Christ's law of love frees us from the multiplicity of rules. But freedom, we soon find, means responsibility—less rules but more restraint.

Resources from which the young Christian can draw strength and wisdom include parents, church, the Bible, other good literature, and the Holy Spirit. When youth finds a reasonable amount of agreement in all these areas, he is less confused in trying to adopt a personal code of behavior.

Most young Christians feel sure that certain things are wrong, but are at a complete loss when asked for a reason. Let us explore further the questions they ask. Here is an excellent letter:

"I have always been fairly popular. But a few weeks ago I was at a party and my friends started dancing, and begged me to dance. I tried to explain that a Christian can do much better things than dancing. I believe when you fill your mind with worldly things you are pulled away from God. I simply could not picture Jesus on the dance floor. I respect my friends because they are a wonderful group. They come to church every time the door is open—sing, usher, and help wherever needed. I have tried to see their side but can't. Please tell me, am I being a fanatic? I believe thousands of other kids are wondering the same thing.   —Girl from Pennsylvania

"I am a Marine, serving overseas. I have a problem and hope you can help me. I like to dance, but my parents don't approve, nor does my girl. She says it is not proper for a Christian to dance. I asked our chaplain and he couldn't help me. Is there something in the Bible about dancing being a sin? I am very anxious to find the answer to this question. I have prayed about it many times, but don't seem to receive an answer."

                                                     —A Marine

There is encouragement in this last letter. Here is a young man, thousands of miles from home, completely free from parental controls, free to do the things he was restrained from doing at home. Yet his early Christian training strongly influences his thinking and acting. Nevertheless, his letter reveals the urgent need for more thorough religious education—the support of reasons rather than mere restrictions. One of the most helpful lessons of all is how to choose right from wrong. This is a major conflict for teens and young adults.

Older Christians should settle on a strong Bible foundation upon which to base their conclusions about standards of behavior. With their own minds clear on New Testament principles, they will understand better what restrictions they need to make. And they can hand down the same stable yardstick for teens to regulate their own choices. Here follows a few pertinent Scripture passages and comments.

Does This Activity Honor Christ?

"So, whether you eat or drink, or whatever you do, do all to the glory of God" (1 Cor. 10:31*).

Does the movie in question honor Christ? Or is it violent, vulgar, and sexy? Is Christ honored at this dance? Is the general atmosphere here Christ-honoring?

How Do You Classify This?

"Now the works of the flesh are plain: immorality, impurity, licentiousness, . . . drunkenness, carousing, and the like. I warn you, as I warned you before, that those who do such things shall not inherit the kingdom of God. But the fruit of the Spirit is love, joy, peace, patience, kindness, goodness, faithfulness, gentleness, self-control; against such there is no law. And those who belong to Christ Jesus have crucified the flesh with its passions and desires" (Gal. 5:19-24*).

Together with your young people, make three lists: *wrong, doubtful,* and *right.* Under *wrong* place activities which you consider taboo for a Christian. Under *right* list all the activities your conscience would sanction as good and safe. Now under *doubtful* enter all the amusements you are uncertain about, the ones which bring a question to your mind. Compare your classification with the Bible verses you have just read. Can you see distinctions between the "fruit of the Spirit" and the "works of the flesh" in relation to decisions facing youth?

Does This Activity Create Moral Problems?

"For the grace of God that bringeth salvation hath appeared to all men, Teaching us that, denying ungodliness and worldly lusts, we should live soberly, righteously, and godly, in this

---

*Scripture passages marked with an asterisk are from the Revised Standard Version of the Holy Bible and are used by permission.

present world" (Tit. 2:11-12). See the rendering in *The Amplified New Testament*.

The close embrace of many kinds of dances may arouse urges or passions that lead to loss of moral controls. Often I hear the comeback: "But it's safer to dance than to park and pet." Why do either? You never know what may happen on the way home from a dance. Physical nearness involved in dancing may enmesh two people before they are aware of the temptation. T. B. Matson in his book *Right or Wrong?* tells of a study made on forty college campuses. "It was found that the more prevalent dancing was on the campus the more prevalent were petting, drinking among both men and women students, and premarital sex relations and even homosexuality."

Will This Activity Hinder My Influence?

"Let no one despise your youth, but set the believers an example in speech and conduct, in love, in faith, in purity" (1 Tim. 4:12*).

Written to a young man nearly two thousand years ago, this counsel speaks just as timely to space-age youth anytime, anywhere. No Christian can honestly ignore the matter of influence. Instead of thinking in terms of Will this hurt me? we had better add: Will this hinder another who may be following in my steps? Paul puts it this way: "But rather decide never to put a stumbling-block or hindrance in the way of a brother" (Rom. 14:13*).

What About the School Prom?

A letter from Oregon voices the query of many Christian teens: "What about junior and senior proms? Many who don't attend other dances go to these. Is there a difference? The school prom is something all the kids look forward to."

The school prom may be the one and only dance for some few, but for most it is only part of the picture. The habit can grow, may lead on to public dance halls and night clubs.

The courageous stand of even one "maximum" Christian girl or fellow can be a mighty support for weak and unsure Christians. I am thinking of a fine Christian young man who was elected president of his large senior class—yet he never attended a school dance.

Some churches with similar ideas on dancing get together to honor their grads at a banquet. The girls get a chance to wear

43

their new formals, complete with corsages from their best beaux. There's music, food, recreation—a night to remember with no regrets. And these sophisticates feel that they have missed out on nothing worthwhile.

How to Refuse

Always teach youth: "In your hearts reverence Christ as Lord." Teach them to look instantly to Christ within for wisdom, courage, and dignity, which will command respect. It is not so much what is said as the manner of saying it, that expresses Christian dignity. The answers to Why don't you dance? What's wrong with dancing? should be given with reverence—reverence for God and also reverence for persons. A young Christian might say something like this: "I just feel that dancing is not the best type of recreation for a Christian. It is not for me to say what you should do, but I must choose what I think is right for me."

Let us not be overanxious to shield our teens from the hardships which normally shape human personality. Unless a child learns early to master the difficult, in later life the difficult may master him. A bit of ridicule will not harm your teen, but instead may help him "endure hardness, as a good soldier of Jesus Christ," making him stronger for the battles ahead. "Indeed all who desire to live a godly life in Christ Jesus will be persecuted" (2 Tim. 3:12*).

Are modern young Christians unwilling to sacrifice? Afraid to be different? Too soft to stand up to their honest beliefs? Are they more eager for popularity in the group than approval of Christ? Are they more concerned with pleasing self than with helping others through leadership and example? Or is it you, fathers and mothers, who are pushing your children in the limelight, afraid they will miss out in the popularity contest?

What about the fond mothers who can scarcely wait for their baby girls to learn ballet, so eager are they for their daughters to develop beauty of form and motion? The ballet training which frees teens from inhibitions may also free them from a proper sense of modesty. Many so-called "charm schools" are definitely misleading—they are only out for the money and have small concern over harmful results and disappointments which often follow. A recent article in a popular magazine warns against being taken in by promises of charm schools.

44

Questions Regarding Dress

Your teens may ask: "Is it wrong to wear makeup and costume jewelry? Should Christian girls wear shorts in public?"

Paul's rule of modesty holds good for the modern girl and woman: "women should adorn themselves modestly and sensibly in seemly apparel . . . as befits women who profess religion" (1 Tim. 2:9-10*). Customs vary widely as to time and place; they are a far cry today from those of two centuries ago. Yet every generation has a valid translation of modesty. Peter speaks of "the imperishable jewel of a gentle and quiet spirit." This jewel shines with the same beauty in godly women today, and the outward expression is a simple loveliness all men admire.

None of us feel called upon or qualified to define modesty for our neighbor. But we cannot but think that many mothers and daughters exhibit a dire lack of propriety in such matters.

Does garish jewelry or excess makeup really become a Christian? How about a decollete gown with dipping neckline or no back? Has the sight of short shorts become so common at all sorts of public places that such attire is proper? Many Christians have become so inured to such styles that they think nothing of them. There's no intention of immodesty—they simply find play clothes comfortable. But we must remember that freedom in Christ carries responsibility to restrict ourselves as worthy examples of our Lord, endeavoring always to follow in his steps.

But, after all, the individual must decide for himself in matters of conscience, things not expressly forbidden in the New Testament. Paul strongly advises that we should avoid offending others and refrain from judging. But this we know: God gives mothers the responsibility to teach modesty to their daughters.

Other Social Practices

"What does the church teach about smoking, social drinking, and card playing? Do you consider these things as worldly pleasure?"

—Youth Leader from Indiana

Spirit-filled leaders have always held a high standard of personal behavior, teaching against practices which are harmful to the body or spirit. Paul Dietzel, outstanding coach, said something like this: "People want to know about our training rules. Well, the training, the want-to must come from within the boys themselves. They know that if they smoke, drink, or gamble they just can't play on our team—they just can't make it. For younger boys athletes are heroes. If they see a favorite athlete breaking rules, smoking, drinking, or gambling, that's quite a letdown."

An excellent approach from a religious standpoint also, don't you think? We may not say, "If you smoke you can't play on our team (be a member of our church)," but the young Christian soon finds that personal discipline is essential if he is to grow toward the measure of the stature of Christ. He wants to be a safe guide for those who are younger in years or new in the Christian faith. As to social drinking, the real Christian stand can never be less than total abstinence—although some popular churches have relaxed their rules to include in their fellowship the social drinker.

The church has always opposed gambling, and card playing still classifies as such. We do not refer to harmless or educational games which utilize some form of cards. But the type of cards associated with gambling has no place in the hands or homes of Christians. Here is a fine place to draw the line for ourselves and our house.

Coach Dietzel is right; outward controls, enforced rules are not enough. The real training must start within. This is our most urgent task as parents and church leaders. We must make doing right so attractive that the desire will be written deep within the minds and emotions of youth.

SUMMING UP

What questions cause your teens greatest concern?

How can Christians approach togetherness on these issues?

Draw up your outline of basic New Testament principles for making choices.

Make three lists of activities: *Wrong, doubtful, right.*

What will you do with *doubtful?*

Teach teens to use resources of a threefold test: spiritual leaders, the Bible, and the Holy Spirit.

Whenever possible, help your teens arrive at their own decisions.

7

The adolescent struggles for independence, verbalizing vehemently his protest against protective ruling of the adult group. He does not want to be told what clothes to wear, what hours to keep, what food to eat, what political party to respect, or what ethical or moral formula to embrace. On the other hand, he is unable to handle his independent activities as adequately as he did in the immediate past. He is impulsive in his behavior and confused about his goals.*

WHY CAN'T I CHOOSE MY FRIENDS?

Your Teens Say

"I am not a Christian but my parents are very religious. I have been dating a boy of sixteen who is a Catholic. I'd like to keep going with him, for he is very nice, but I won't be able to if my parents find out he's Catholic. I see nothing wrong so long as we are not serious."

—Girl from West Virginia

"Some time ago I asked advice about breaking up with a boy who was not Christian nor interested in becoming one. I did break up with him, but here's my trouble—the influence of him and other friends has rubbed off on me, and I have picked up some of their habits, like cursing. But I do not wish to do this; please pray for God to help me quit."

—Girl from Ohio

"I'm all mixed up on what to do. I'm married and have a child, and love my husband very much. But he drinks, especially when things do not go his way. Now he tells me that we have been raised far too differently ever to get along. Yet he says, 'I can't live with you and I can't live without you.' What can I do?"

—Young Woman from Kansas

---

*From *The Adolescent and His World*, Josselyn, p. 38.

"Before my salvation I ran around with a bad crowd. This was a very crucial time in my life—my early teens. Although I finally broke away from this gang, I'm afraid it was too late, for their influence has made a deep mold on my character. For some time now I have been dating a fine Christian boy, thinking we could help each other. But instead, I feel sure that I make him sex conscious, and I'm afraid my emotions will get out of control. Please help me."

—Girl from the East

"If I am accepted I shall soon enter one of our church colleges to prepare for the ministry. For over a year I have been going with a girl from another church. She does not profess to be a Christian but says she will become one for my sake. Is this the girl for me?"

—Boy from Pennsylvania

"I am nineteen and a college student. Ever since I can remember I have gone to church and tried to live as good a Christian life as I could. In one article you told of girls who ask: 'Where are boys who act like Christians?' I think the shoe belongs on the other foot. I'd like to know where these girls exist. The church girls I know prefer dating boys who drink a little and have traffic arrests by the gross. I don't believe in dating people outside the church because they expect you to attend dances and drink—and more; I've found this out for a fact. Meanwhile, I'm without a girl friend, while the girls in my group date other fellows."

—Boy from West Virginia

Often a parent is greatly disturbed over the marriage of a son or daughter to one of a completely different background and culture. "I can only blame myself," a father admitted sadly. "All his life I taught my child against every kind of discrimination. And he took me at my word. Sure, I was right teaching him to love his neighbor as himself. But I failed to teach him the fine art of discrimination—in selecting a life mate." Marriage advisors agree that similarity of background, education, religion, and family customs makes for happier marriages.

Why Not Date a Catholic?

"Jon must be a sincere Christian," Maybeth told her mother. "He's far more loyal to his church than most Protestants I know.

Why, he wouldn't think of eating meat on Friday, and he never misses early Sunday morning mass. Imagine me getting up at five!"

"Or even eight," the mother added. "But, Maybeth, the very fact that Jon is so loyal to his church worries me. I know now that I should never have let you start dating Jon; the differences [in your beliefs] are just too great."

"But, Mother, if we are both sincere in our religion, I see no reason why we could not make a happy marriage. We're alike in many other ways—and you know I'll never turn Catholic. You needn't worry about that."

Later this couple became engaged. Jon said cautiously, "Before we make any plans, Maybeth, we'll have to see my priest and talk with him. You don't mind, do you?"

"Why, no, Jon, of course not. I'd love to meet your priest. You met my pastor at my house one evening."

Maybeth was a bit troubled to learn from the priest that she must go to him for at least six lessons on Roman Catholic theology. They must be married by no one but a priest, and she would be required to sign a document—otherwise Jon would be excommunicated from his church. After the third lesson Maybeth came away with a copy of this document.

It was at this point that Maybeth decided to talk with her own pastor. Together they read the fine print of the "Ante-Nuptial Agreement," which a non-Catholic must sign when marrying a Catholic. Section 2 read:

"The parties severally and mutually promise without any reservations, tacit or expressed, that all children of either sex born of this marriage, shall be baptized only in the Roman Catholic Church, and shall be educated only in the Roman Catholic faith, according to the teachings of the Roman Catholic Church, in a Catholic school whenever possible."

"Maybeth, is this what you want?" Pastor Brown asked with deep concern.

"I don't know, Pastor Brown . . ." Maybeth stammered, "I'd surely want to take my children with me to church . . . I'd want our whole family to worship together—at least part of the time."

"But that can never be," Pastor Brown said sadly shaking his head. "And notice number three. You promise that you 'shall in no way interfere with the party of the second part [Jon] in the free exercise of religion.' You agree to carry out all these promises—rear your children Catholic—even if Jon should die . . . and there's much more. Jon vows to do all in his power to bring about your conversion."

"My conversion!" Maybeth cried, "It's all unfair! I've just as much right to make such demands of Jon. Can Jon really want all this?"

"Perhaps not," Pastor Brown agreed, "but what can he do? He's under the power of the Pope of Rome, and these are his orders. Suppose you tell Jon that your pastor requires your fiance to take six lessons on the doctrines of the New Testament as your church sees it. As your pastor, Maybeth, I do demand this—with your consent, of course. Okay?"

"Okay, I'll do it! I'll tell Jon that my minister demands that *he* take instruction in my faith—that *he* must sign a paper promising that our children may go to my church at least half the time. You fix up the paper, and I'll take it to him. That's more than fair."

"I'll bring the papers to you in the morning," Pastor Brown promised. "Are you sure, Maybeth, that you want to go through with this?"

"Yes, Pastor, I know the risks. But if Jon and I cannot come to a reasonable agreement, we'd better know it now. A completely one-sided marriage is not my idea of mutual happiness." Maybeth arose to leave the study.

Next evening when her fiance came by for their visit to the priest, Maybeth handed him the papers. The usual calm fellow bit his lips, frowning.

"Maybeth," he chose his words carefully. "I know this is hard for you to understand, but it's different with Catholics. You see, we believe that the Catholic Church is the only true church, the one established by Jesus Christ himself. That's why it would be a mortal sin for me to do what you ask—not that I think it unreasonable from your viewpoint. Maybe it's a sin for me to say so, but I wish I were free to go with you to your church. Yet, as a loyal Catholic it's out of the question."

"But, Jon, is it fair for me to make all the concessions? Must I sign away all my rights and privileges to the Catholic Church while my husband and children are forbidden to enter my church?"

"I'm sorry, Maybeth; you know I love you but—well, I had hoped you would some day see my way."

50

"Listen, Jon, I feel just as strongly about my religion as you do yours. I know that I have been 'born again'; I know when Christ came into my heart and became my personal Savior. Could I renounce all this and sign the oath your church demands? Read this: 'I now with grief and contrition for my past errors, profess that I believe the Holy, Catholic, Apostolic Roman Church to be the only true church established on earth by Jesus Christ, to which I submit myself with my whole heart . . .'"

"After you learn more about my church, you'll feel different, Maybeth. Why not give it a try at least?"

"No, Jon. The fact is I had hoped you would see the truth. I see now how very wrong it would be for me to vow and sign my unborn children over to a church and system of education which I can never accept for myself. Can't you see the unfairness, Jon, the—"

"I'm sorry, Maybeth, but I didn't make the rules. I just obey them."

"I'm sorry, too," Maybeth spoke as if a load had suddenly lifted. "I know now for certain that you and I could not hope for a Christian marriage, a Christian home and family. I don't believe in the Catholic Church, and I shall never obey its rules. But I shall pray for you, Jon. I pray with all my heart that some day you will assert your freedom—as you would really like to do. Until then, good-bye, Jon, good-bye . . ."

Why Not Date a Non-Christian?

"Do not be mismated with unbelievers. For what partnership have righteousness and iniquity? Of what fellowship has light with darkness" (2 Cor. 6:14*)?

There is always the possibility of a partner for a *date* turning into a partner for a *mate*. When I asked a youth group at a convention: "What do you think about dating non-Christians?" one fellow gave a good answer. "When I think of dating a girl," he said, "I always ask myself, 'What kind of wife would she make?' I don't care to date someone I feel sure I would never wish to marry."

Of course, a casual date now and then is not the same as regular dating. But the casual date can quickly become something more. A girl who appears so correct around adults may be the kind who makes a fellow sex conscious. She may be quite persuasive in her determination to drive to a night club just for a kick.

Parents who care about their daughters insist upon knowing something about the young man who asks for a date. Does he smoke? Drink? Use foul language? What sort of home does he come from? Does he hold to a high moral standard? Is he a safe driver? Is he a responsible student.

What's Wrong with the Gang?

Usually we think a young couple is safer in group dating than going off alone. But this is not true with an irresponsible group —dangers to life and morals are multiplied by a wild gang determined to flout home controls and church standards. Adults may not pose as chaperones, but they must still supervise teens in their sports, parties, and motor trips.

Double-dating may double the pleasure and security of young pairs—but not always. Heavy petting going on in the back seat of the car may start reactions in the more discreet couple.

One recognized authority says to fathers: "Know your son's friends, and don't allow floaters at parties. Pleasant, affectionate, firm insistence on considerate behavior and acceptance of responsibility is all that will see you through these difficult years."

Why Didn't You Tell Me?

"I wish you and Dad had told me more about how you felt about such things as divorce before I left home," a young man wrote his mother. "Maybe then I would not have become involved with a girl who has been married and has a child—I didn't realize you had such strong objections to divorce. Anyway, it's too late now; I couldn't bear to hurt Sherrie—she has suffered too much already, through no fault of her own. I'm sorry to disappoint you, and I do hope you can accept and love Sherrie when you get to know her."

Opportunities for establishing patterns and setting standards— how quickly they pass! Where were you when this romance was budding—this one which is causing you so much grief and guilt? Even when unfortunate friendships have been made, parents may still take steps to provide alternatives. First of all, face the facts; discover where you have failed as a parent. Have you been too busy to entertain your teens' friends at home? Have you turned your young people loose to seek out their own means of having fun?

Often youngsters discover a friend's undesirable traits when this person is exposed to a better atmosphere. A mother was advised to set up an evening party of Christian young people to which her son's friend, a rather wild Jane, had been invited. The contrast with the more refined girls was too obvious for the son to miss. And the friendship came to a close. Other steps may be taken to introduce new interests and involve new acquaintances—a hobby, a part-time job, more family activities, a vacation trip, a youth camp.

An alert church-school teacher or youth director should quickly spot teen alliances which may spell trouble for one or both young people. Together with parents, they may be able to quietly bring about changes—without rousing teens to revolt.

Summing Up

When is group dating safe? What advantages?

When is double-dating safe?

Why not date a Catholic?

Why date only Christians?

Is the church making clear the Bible position on divorce?

How can you help "undesirable friends" without harming your own teens?

How teach teens to rightly discriminate?

How change wrong friendships?

8

It was the policy of the good old gentleman to make his children feel that home was the happiest place in the world; and I value this delicious home-feeling as one of the choicest gifts a parent can bestow.—Washington Irving

NO FUN AT OUR HOUSE

Your Girls Say

"I have fine Christian parents and a brother whom I love very much, but lately I find it hard to communicate with my parents. It seems that I have drifted away from them. I can't talk to my mother confidentially because I no longer feel close to her as I once did. I try my best to get along with my brother, but everything I do is wrong. My father is quite understanding and I love him very much, and I'd do anything to have the close relationship restored between my mother and me."

"Things are in a terrible mess at my house. My father is very set in his ways and never tries to understand my sister and me [both are teens]. I study hard and think I could make better grades at school if I was sure my father would not beat me or talk to my teacher. Mom acts as if she is afraid of Dad, too. We've been going to the same church for many years, but since the church has installed a kitchen, Dad won't let us go there any more. Must I lose all my friends?"

"Recently I gave my life to Christ, and I admit that my greatest weakness is my awful temper. I say things I don't mean because deep inside something tells me that Mom does not see my side in anything. There is much quarreling between us, and I resent everything she says because she treats me like a baby. I'm thirteen and still have a lot to learn, but I don't think I'm always wrong."

"How can a girl of fifteen or sixteen years old find a place to stay? I don't want to live where I am not wanted and am treated like a servant—expected to do all the housework and wait on my brothers hand and foot."

"Dad acts like a dictator over Mom and us children. We disagree on many religious subjects also, and there are arguments and ill feelings among the whole family."

"I wish my parents would take time for some family fun at least once a week. But they say they are too busy working to provide us with the things we need. I'd be willing to get along with less so that we could enjoy our home and family more."

Your Boys Say

"I'm old enough to make a few decisions of my own, but my parents insist on running my life. I'm thinking of leaving home."

"I try to live as a Christian should, but nothing I ever do pleases my dad. How can I make him see that I am trying to do my best?"

"My parents gave me permission to play on the high school football team. But when I have to stay after school to practice, they always accuse me of loitering on my way home. They say I'm just trying to get out of work—which is not true."

"I'd like to bring some of my friends home now and then—both boys and girls. But my mother says it's too much trouble, and that we can't afford parties."

This Worked Out

"I know I'm young, but I look years older than my age," began the first letter from unhappy Luana, aged fourteen. "I've talked with my parents about dating, but they don't seem to understand. They simply refuse to let me date. So I've been sneaking out and going with a boy who is very nice. We both know we shouldn't date behind my parents' backs, but I feel that they are in the wrong. If only they would let us go together to church or to a skating party, we would be careful to come in at the time they set. How can I make them understand?"

I wrote back: "You can't, not by sneaking out on them. The only way is to make parents see with their own eyes that you are growing up. First of all, prove to them that they can trust you. You haven't, you know. . . . Show your parents that you know how to behave. Convince them—with a little patience and time."

Luana flashed back: "I am so very happy that I decided to write you because the minute I got your answer I knew you were right. My boyfriend and I had a long talk about our secret dating, and we decided to break up and just be good friends. Of course, I feel the same way about him, but I'm sure

55

it's better this way. I'm still afraid to tell my father about this boy, but I feel it would be the right thing to do. What do you think?"

Quickly I replied: "No doubt you will feel better to make a clean sweep of the whole affair. Of course, your dad may scold a bit—really, he has cause, you know—but you can take it. And I think you both will feel closer after that. . . . I'm sure, Luana, you already know what you really want to do."

The final letter: "I decided that having a talk with Dad was the right thing to do, so I told him everything. We had several long talks, and he said he was glad I trusted him enough to confide in him. Even though some of my privileges have been taken away for a while, things are working out for good. I believe the Lord has shown me the right path to take. Thanks so much!"

She Saw the Light

"I thought of the wonderful evening I had spent with Bob as we rounded the corner of Church and Elm Streets. For months I'd wanted to date Bob, and finally he had asked me to go roller skating. We'd had a great time.

"Driving up in front of the house, we lingered in the car talking about the evening, when to my horror the porch light started to flash on and off. 'Oh, no!' I thought to myself, 'not Dad flashing that porch light again.' I knew he didn't want me to sit in the car with fellows, but after all, I was only talking. Against my best judgment, I ignored the signal.

"In about ten minutes the light started flashing again, accompanied by a head peering around the blind. This time I was mortified and so was Bob. 'What's the matter with your Dad?' he said in a hurt tone, 'It looks as if he can't trust me with his daughter.' I was practically in tears as Bob escorted me in great haste to my door and was gone before I had thanked him for the evening. My life was ruined!

"As I stepped inside I exploded. 'The idea of flashing that light on and off! Can't I talk for one minute with my date without having him insulted?'

"Instead of Dad shouting back at me, he just let me go on ranting. When I hushed, he said quietly, 'Sit down, Nancy, and we'll talk this over.'

"First he let me present my side of the story—this time calmly.

I explained how he made me feel that he didn't trust me, as if he thought I was doing something wrong, and how he offended Bob. Then Dad said he hadn't realized how I felt about the matter and that he was sorry to have embarrassed me before Bob. He said that he knew that I was just talking, but since neighbors might not understand, I must be more careful. Also he made it plain that I was not to sit in a parked car—for reasons he enumerated. By talking things out this way, we came to a definite understanding. And I promised Dad that the next time I'd remember: I must not only *be* good, I must *look* good."

Your Teens' Rights

Children have no choice in the sort of climate which will mold their future. Short of gross neglect and brutality, they are supposed to take what their home gives, and like it. Nevertheless, parents have strict orders from God: "And, ye fathers, provoke not your children to wrath: but bring them up in the nurture and admonition of the Lord" (Eph. 6:4). J. B. Phillips renders the verse: "Fathers, don't overcorrect your children or make it difficult for them to obey the commandment. Bring them up with Christian teaching in Christian discipline."

"Nurture" is a good word; it suggests: train, sustain, support, discipline, and prepare. In the spirit of a true father, Paul said to one church: "But we were gentle among you, even as a nurse cherisheth her children" (1 Thess. 2:7).

Christian Discipline

Do you think of discipline only in terms of punishment? It includes much more, in fact the whole area of training and preparing for mature living. And we know it takes time to grow a responsible human being.

Punishment for misdeeds is a necessary part of the upbringing of the average child. This may take the form of restraint, of deprivation, or even pain inflicted by a smooth, slender switch on tender legs. But the use of force serves little purpose with teens. Having been brought up in Christian nurture, they will respond to a more mature discipline, administered in the firm but loving terms of a few governing rules—with appropriate penalties for breaking of them. Make these rules unmistakably clear. Too often a teen does not really know what his father and mother expect of him. Parents themselves may have no clearly outlined set of ideals by which to direct their family.

A Christian Climate

The climate is more important in nurture than any set of rules. After the death of a beloved husband, the wife and mother withdrew into a shell of morbid grief. Although she did not mean to be selfish, she went all out in the performing of duties in caring for her fatherless children. But can you picture a home where for years the children never once saw their mother smile? Children have a right to all the happiness a loving home can afford—and no home where Christ abides should be short on the sunshine and laughter of real joy.

Think of the distraught nerves and troubled minds of young people in a house (not a real home) of contention and strife. Here parents show no kindness and affection for each other.

The Christian climate is one of peace and joy, of firm Christian principles, of prayer and worship, of guidance and instruction, of counseling together in a spirit of understanding and humility.

The Family Council

Wisdom and humility are excellent qualifications for a successful family council. Each member is given a chance to express his opinions and to offer suggestions. Each contribution is respected and given careful consideration. The family may discuss sharing in home duties and starting new projects, as well as interests in recreation or cultural arts. They may put their heads together and come up with a code to govern dating habits. Often misunderstandings need clearing. Dad or Mom may acknowledge, "I was at fault; I made a mistake." Group participation, so valuable in adult life, begins in the family circle.

Self-Discipline

The real purpose of home discipline is to build within the youth self-discipline, the ability to know right from wrong, and the will to choose the right. By regular church going, participating in group worship, supporting the program in all the areas of stewardship, the family grows together in happy realtionships with each other, with the church, and with God.

In his small book *Discipline and Discovery* Albert Edward Day sets forth the first aim thus: "To seek for ourselves the highest New Testament standard of Christian experience and life." This is to be attained through personal disciplines of

58

obedience, simplicity, humility, frugality, generosity, charity, truthfulness, and purity. A family may journey together in seeking to practice these disciplines of the spiritual life.

Never has youth needed so urgently solid homes where abide faith, hope, and charity. Never was the need greater for faith in the Bible, faith in the church, faith in Christ as Lord and Savior, faith in the power and goodness of God. Never was the need greater for the eternal hope, based on personal acquaintance with Christ, and never the need so great for that charity, that love which serves God "in justice, fortitude of soul, and humility."

Living in a world of uncertainties and threats, parents still must infuse in youth a love for living. We need to encourage young people to go on dreaming and planning, to go on developing to the full their God-given abilities. Each day our grandmothers were careful to save over enough yeast for the making of tomorrow's batch of dough. Likewise, we must preserve the joy of living, whatever ills overtake our family. This is part of our daily bread. If the joy of the Lord keeps bubbling in the hearts of mother and father, it will spread like a leaven throughout the house.

Summing Up

Analyze youth's need of protective discipline, restraint of wrong behavior, praise for the good.

How can you best support a teen who has a problem?

Does understanding the teen's viewpoint necessarily mean agreeing with that viewpoint?

What is the relationship of developing self-direction to that of self-discipline?

What are benefits of group participation in the family?

How do these experiences develop leadership?

Does being an understanding parent mean abdicating authority?

Explore ways of cultivating a love for living.

Think of ways of bringing about closer fellowship between the parents in a home.

9

You cannot educate without discipline. . . . These three things—excellence, discipline and faith—are the very business of education.—James P. Mitchell

WHICH VOCATION FITS ME?

Mr. Mitchell, who was Secretary of Labor under President Eisenhower, urged that training for a vocation be started early. He says: "Even senior high school may be too late. Preparation must be made in the junior high schools. Or, in their embryonic form, in the elementary grades."

Your Teens Say

"I have given my life to Christ for him to control. When finishing elementary school I asked God to show me his will for my life, and after praying consistently for six months, I had my answer. God showed me that through a terrific struggle I will finally succeed in becoming a doctor. Since I was knee-high to a duck I was always interested in the scientific field. I have taken vocational tests and ability and aptitude tests. These were interpreted by a reliable counselor who agrees that I should be able to become a doctor. But so far my academic record does not prove it. I am still trying and I know God will open a way because I am in his hands."

—Boy from the North

"The biggest decision in my life has troubled me more than anything else in all my sixteen and a half years. Two years ago, when I was a freshman, the big question among the girls was 'What am I going to do with my life?' I had thought about many things; teacher, nurse, missionary, even a politician. I was certain that I should not be a missionary unless God gave me a definite call. Then last summer our Youth Fellowship had a spiritual inventory retreat at a park in our city. When a powerful youth minister was speaking, I felt closer to God than ever before. In the evening service as the sun was setting and the sky was scarlet, a stream of yellow rays broke through and Christ spoke to my heart saying, 'Go ye therefore and teach all nations . . . and, lo, I am with you alway, even to the end of the world. So on that day I felt God had called me to be a missionary. I began planning to go to a church college and am still counting on this. But I have a feeling that something is not quite right. I do need help because that feeling is awful."

—Girl from the Midwest

"Soon I will be out of the Army, and my future is one big question mark. How shall I prepare for God's service?"

—Boy in Service

"Recently I made my final dedication to the Lord. He knows that I now mean business. Missions lay heavily on my heart and after much searching and prayer, this is the work I feel God would have me do. And so I am preparing to do Bible translating among peoples who have no written language. This summer I am attending a Summer Institute of Linguistics. I enlist your prayers that I may take all the rest of the steps in the will of God."

—Boy from the West

"I know why I'm here and where I'm going." How few individuals can confidently make this assertion. How few discover in their young adulthood a satisfying concept of God, his purpose for their existence, and his plan for their lives. Fortunate is the young man or woman whose parents exhibit a life-faith in purposeful living. As Dr. Benjamin Spock says, "He [the youth] secretly borrows from their strength of purpose until he can develop his own."

This morning I was talking with a consulting scientist of a large corporation which does research in technical instruments for medical science and nuclear devices. Because he is one of the "boys" from our church, we are justifiably proud of his achievements. This young man says that more than anything else the study of physics has confirmed his faith in God and the Bible. Moreover, he acknowledges his dependence on the Holy Spirit for that extra-plus needed in all human endeavor. He believes that God will guide in the pursuit of any vocation that merits his approval.

Thoughtful parents are concerned about their children's future, but too often little consideration is given to the children's interests or abilities. As a result parents insist on a career to gratify their own ambitions. One brilliant couple, hoping their son would choose either law or medicine, pressured him through high school. But after several years of frustrating experiences, the parents have become reconciled to a far different role for their son—one in which he can find satisfaction and a measure of usefulness. A frank evaluation of the boy's natural inclinations and mental powers might have spared them all this disappointment.

Every youth faces the problem of deciding what sort of person he wants to be. He must discover his own basic interests, his abilities, and work attitudes in time to make his best preparation. He needs an abundance of guidance but also a measure of freedom in selecting the elements out of which he will fashion a life career. For a time he may appear fickle while his interests and hobbies skip from scientific experimenting to raising frogs. The growing-up years bring frequent shifts in personality, interests, and activities; he tries out first one job and then another. Choosing the vocation which will best fit is no easy task for the young adult.

The average high school student is likely thinking: "Don't know what I want to do, what I can do, or how to get started." Where can he turn for help? The school counseling program in cooperation with your employment service aims to help each student build a vocational plan, a sort of tentative goal to guide him. So that he can discover his own basic gifts and desires, he will be given various standard tests: vocational interest inventory, vocational aptitude test, personality adjustment inventory, and intelligence tests. An overall counseling program enables the high school student to choose:

1. *A job he can do.* He discovers himself—his mental abilities and potential skills, his strongest subjects, and his weakest points.

2. *A job he will like.* This takes into consideration his interests, associates, salary, promotional opportunities, and the effects on home and family life.

3. *A job that gives satisfaction.* The job must be in keeping with religious ideals. It must provide a sense of worthy achievement, and it should allow time for free participation in the program of the church.

Young men face such urgent questions as: Shall I go on to

college now, work a while first, get married, or serve a hitch in the Army? Girls also face decisions about launching a career, completing education, or getting married. The Bureau of Labor has issued an *Occupational Outlook Handbook*. Listed in it are some four hundred occupations best suited to women. But regardless of circumstances, a vocational plan helps to steady the young adult through these uncertain years.

To know God early is important. Children who experience conversion are better able to grasp a satisfying concept of God and his plan for their lives. It is not enough to ask, "What do I want to do?" There can be many conflicting answers. The Christian asks urgently, "Lord, what have you planned for my life?" A full-time Christian lives and works full time for God—whether he is a doctor, lawyer, farmer, or preacher.

Recently a young man asked, "How can I do all to the glory of God? When I go fishing, I don't fish to honor God." But, why not? If you're catching fish for a living, you can do that to the glory of God. But more likely you go fishing for the mere pleasure of it. Well, a Christian needs recreation, and surely he can worship God on a fishing outing. Christ loved to follow his men about the Sea of Galilee; he even told them where to cast nets.

Brother Lawrence used to say, "The time of business does not differ with me from the time of prayer." He served God as well in the kitchen as he did on his knees in church. Parents and church leaders hope to demonstrate this attitude and practice before their youth. They wish them to grow up in a Christ-centered atmosphere that they may early surrender to God's will and learn his ways of working and guiding in each individual life.

Every young Christian faces the possibility of a call to a full-time church vocation. Before deciding upon his lifework the young adult should spend time on his knees talking it over with God and listening for divine direction. If one feels an insistent leading over a long period of time toward a Christian ministry, he should consult with spiritual advisers. When one sees clearly a great need, sees his own ability to fit that need, and feels that he *must* do something about it—then he should make himself available. He can begin to prepare by entering college or working toward the goal. He can study at home, and he can work at small tasks which come to hand. He can volunteer for minor responsibilities in the church program, and he can witness for Christ person to person.

On the other hand, the vocation which concerns the young Christian may be one normally classified as secular. But this, too, deserves his most prayerful consideration, for he can be sure that God has promised the guidance needed. Some careers offer more opportunity for Christian service than others. We list a few of these:

Teaching should perhaps stand second only to preaching. The teaching ministry offers vast avenues for training young minds. Outside of parents, no one else has so many chances for influencing children and youth as the Christian teacher.

Counseling, closely related to teaching and preaching, renders vital service to youth and family. Every pastor is of necessity a counselor, and for this role he has access to books such as these: *Pastoral Counseling*, by Seward Hiltner, and *The Psychology of Counseling*, by Clyde M. Narramore. Young people who have the ability and aptitude will do well to consider this profession.

Medicine appeals to Christian youth who have the urge to minister to man's bodily ills along with his mental and spiritual needs. Countless areas in research call also to the young man or woman who is willing to give long years in preparation and continued study and sacrificial work. Nursing (close related) provides real Christian service for men as well as women.

Business offers two unique opportunities: (1) the chance to carry Christ into the business world, to witness for him to men of the world, (2) the venture to act as stewards in using money and position to carry out Christ's commission of world evangelization. But one needs to take into account the temptations which accompany wealth and honor, the risk of self-seeking instead of Christ-motivating in everything.

Social work challenges many to a relatively new type of Christian vocation. Special preparation is needed—graduate study in sociology, social science, counseling, and psychology. The professional social worker has a broad field to choose from, including work among mentally retarded children and adults, juvenile delinquents, alcoholics, welfare services, family service, and a variety of hospital positions.

Journalism invites the Christian who has gifts to dedicate to feature writing, free-lance writing, fictional writing, proof reading, photography, editing, and publishing. The student who loves to write and whose efforts merit praise from his teachers may break into this field by mailing a letter now and then to his local newspaper. He may send in a report of youth activities to his church weekly. He may never be more than a part-time writer; his monetary gains may be small, but his work will be highly rewarding.

Ministry now includes full-time vocations of Christian service in several fields, such as pastoral ministry, evangelism, missions in the homeland and abroad, medical missions—including nursing, Christian education, ministry of music, counseling, and youth ministry.

The Problem Stated in clear terms will be a big step toward solution. Our complex economy boasts of about thirty-five thousand different identifiable occupations. While one cannot hope to survey them all, he can at least scan the major fields which seem most appealing. Here is one method of stating this problem:

1. Looking over the major work opportunities, ask prayerfully, Where is the neediest field for Christian effort?

2. Choose two or three specific vocations which appear most urgent. List them in order of their importance.

3. Survey your potential abilities; write out a statement of your gifts and qualifications, even smallest talents.

4. Present these "assets" to God in prayer—to use *where* and *how* he chooses. Lay before him the two lists: the vocations and your gifts. Ask the Holy Spirit to clear your thinking and to make his will plain.

Roles of Parents and Church Leaders

Some families inspire their children to "great heights of personal performance." John W. Gardner* says, "Talent without motivation is inert and of little use in the world." The desire to excel in the face of obstacles, the unflagging zeal to develop abilities and gifts to the utmost—who will provide the motivation? Often when parents fail to expect any degree of excellence in a youth, it is the teacher, youth leader, or pastor who supplies the encouragement, the needed motivation to wake up the apathetic student. "The only limits are one's interest and

---

*From *Excellence,* copyright, 1961, by John W. Gardner (Harper & Brothers, New York). Used by permission of Mr. Gardner.

ability." We can do nothing about ability, but we can challenge interest at every level of ability. We must take into account individual differences, encourage only the goals within reach, but every high school graduate can "profit by continued education of *some* kind." If college is not within his capacity, there are many other training programs to pursue. To mention a few: night classes, apprenticeships, special schools (music, nursing, business, art), correspondence courses, the Armed Services.

"Some people may have greatness thrust upon them. Very few have excellence thrust upon them. They achieve it. They don't stumble into it in the course of amusing themselves. All excellence involves discipline and tenacity of purpose. We must, in short, create conditions that challenge the individual. It is a healthy thing for the young person to face *some kinds* of difficulties, to have to struggle to surmount them, and to learn in the process the values of endurance, courage and strength of purpose."

The general attitude of society has been that a child should never be faced with severe challenge, never be called upon for even minor sacrifices. Is it any wonder that so many fail to meet the tests when faced with the disciplines and rigors of college or the Armed Forces?

Parents, pastors, and other leaders of youth must provide the information, the motivation, and the examples which will help the young adult find himself and his place in God's world here and now. But when others have helped in every way possible, they must stand by and wait for the young adult to give his own answer. "Where will my life count for the most?" This is the supreme decision of the Christian student.

Summing Up

Help a teen discover his real interests.
    Does he like to build with his hands?
    Draw a picture?
    Take a motor apart?
    Experiment with chemicals?
    Nurse a sick dog back to health?
Encourage the use of vocational tests.
Lead teens to investigate possibilities.
Lead them to complete dedication to God.
Teach them dependence on Holy Spirit guidance.

66

Do not pressure them or try to choose for them.
Counsel the teen to choose:

1. A job he can do.
2. A job he will like
3. A job that gives satisfaction
4. A job in which he feels Spirit-led

Specific Role of Parents, Leaders

Recognize individual differences
Provide information
Provide motivation
Provide opportunities
Expect excellence on his level

10

From my experience, not one in twenty marries the first love; we build statues of snow, and weep to see them melt.—Walter Scott

READY FOR SERIOUS DATING

Your Teens Say

"I have been going steady with a boy for some time, and he has asked me to marry him. But now he says he wants to break up. I love him very much and feel that I can never be happy with anyone else. Should I continue writing to give him another chance?"

"Have you ever loved someone so much that when you see him with someone else, you break down in tears? If only somebody understood the way I feel, but it seems as if no one loves me any more."

"I was going with a boy, but we broke up; now I'm going steady with another. But I still like the first one and he wants to go with me again. The trouble is, this second boy is in our way, for we are practically engaged, and I don't know what to say to him. I know I'd rather marry the first boy because I am still in love with him. Please tell me what to do."

"I'm fifteen and going steady with a twenty-year-old non-Christian. I've tried to tell him that I'm too young, but it would break my heart to give him up."

"Is it right for a girl to ask to go steady with a boy when she knows he likes her?"

The later teens are the years for getting ready for marriage, but marriage is not for teen-agers. It is definitely an adult affair with adult responsibilities. Nevertheless, teen marriages are more popular now than in Grandmother's day. The swing has been toward younger marriages, with a corresponding increase in divorce. One writer says that the "D Bomb" in America, the Divorce Boom, is a greater threat than the nuclear bomb.

What of Going Steady?

Let's face it. Most mothers are romantic, almost as much so as their teen daughters. Fine and good! But when Susie comes home with Sam's class ring dangling on a chain, Mom is likely to read more meaning into the symbol than the couple intend. Most boys resent being taken for granted when mothers start treating them like family.

Dads are quite vulnerable too. Susie can tweedle Dad around her little finger when she remembers to use her sweet young charms. He knows that his daughter is too young to go out riding alone with Sam, but then how can he refuse?

"Just what does going steady involve?" one mother asked her fifteen-year-old daughter.

"Why, just—going steady," the girl replied.

The mother learned it meant just that—after giving her consent and making it official. This mother says, "When they are not in school or asleep, they are together! When he can get money for gas and the family car, they go riding, but most of the time they are together in our home or his. Good experience in learning to get along with another family and to become adjusted to the varying moods of a steady"—that is this mother's opinion. But isn't the young couple missing out on other valuable experiences? And why take shortcuts into adulthood? After all, young love, though sweet, seldom develops into a permanent affection.

A Standard to Judge By

Before going steady a girl or boy should have had sufficient dating experience to know how to pick a steady dating partner. Dating intelligence is not something you are born with—it must be acquired through some of the most exciting years of life. Not that a teen's life is all joy, far from it. As one teen said, "Dating is heartbreak, despair, and yet it's heaven!"

It is the role of parents and church leaders to help a teen establish a standard to judge by, to help him think through the general type of person best suited to his own personality and needs. Broadly, a Christian youth wants someone he can admire, respect, and love, one whose backgrounds are similar—educationally, economically, and religiously.

Of course, there are exceptions to most rules; a boy or girl with a most undesirable background may prove to be a person of strong character. But it is not asking too much that he be given time to prove his stability.

Purpose of Steady Dating

When your older teens *think* they are in love, they need to put this love through the time test. Regardless of how strongly they are attracted to each other, they should be sensible enough to drop a love affair which shows no promise of a happy marriage. The time test may vary from a few months to a couple years. If after a short period one or the other discovers that they are unsuited, there is no reason to continue steady dating. Better to break off before they become more deeply involved.

On the other hand, a long period of going steady is preferable to a long engagement. Girls, in particular, find it more complicated to break off an engagement and more difficult to get back into circulation.

Drawbacks to Steady Dating

Many steady daters have no intention of becoming serious, but are only keeping step with a teen fad. Both boys and girls experience a degree of security with a steady for school and church affairs. Girls, especially, consider going steady a door to independence. One girl said, "It's the summit! You break away from parental controls and are really grown-up."

Another reason some couples decide to go steady is that more intimacies are expected. This varies all the way from a light caress to "loving completely." From letters they write, some teens honestly believe that going steady is synonymous with heavy petting—and more—"I am fifteen and a boy who is twenty has asked me to go steady. I would like to know just what is meant by 'petting' and how to prevent getting pregnant. I am trying my best to be a Christian."

Better Investigate

When your teen shows interest in that fascinating new girl or handsome stranger, better do a little private detective work before they become entangled. Christian leaders, including parents, have a difficult role; we teach our children to love everybody alike, to treat all the same. Then suddenly we almost reverse ourselves: Choose your friends carefully. Avoid fellows and girls who have a poor reputation or who have been in trouble; better date only Christians. We have no wish to unchristianize youth by turning them into intolerant snobs, but we can't afford to forget Paul's warning: "Evil companionships, . . . corrupt and deprave good manners and morals and character" (1 Cor. 15:33, *Amplified New Testament*).

How Steady?

Going steady holds different meanings for each couple, for various ages and groups, and for their adult leaders. Some very young couples are quite content to go steady by phone. Every night *he* calls *her* and they discuss current interest of school and church. No dates. Just talking by phone. Parents shouldn't complain too much. After all, this is good training in conversational art which can make later dating more smooth. For the extremely shy boy or girl who writes that he just can't talk on a date, I recommend this as a helpful exercise.

Teen language and customs are almost as variable as the moon, but at this moment, so I am told, *going-steadily* is a part-time arrangement. *He* escorts *her* to all school functions and to other certain affairs as agreed upon. The rest of the time each is free to date whom he pleases.

Many couples go steady without any formality of promise. They date no one else until they tire of each other—less binding but less secure. Others go steady—with all the implications—yet change partners often. They are not really serious. They are only playing a game, but obviously a dangerous one to emotions and perhaps even to morals.

What Can Parents Do?

When fourteen- to sixteen- year-olds insist on freedom to go steady like an engaged couple, should parents simply abandon controls? Many do, but they shirk spiritual and moral obligations imposed by the Lord, civil authorities, and society. Give your teens both trust and protection. Let them know that you do believe in them and that you fully expect them to do the right thing even when out of your sight. At the same time give them the assurance of your continued protection through limits you will still require. You dare not abdicate authority; God holds you responsible.

There may be certain occasions when a young couple of this age may well go out alone. But late night rides or long rides duet style any time of day are out for them. Let them know that a measure of freedom can be earned only through complying with the rules of the home. But always that freedom must be geared to each one's measure of maturity.

Giving advice may sound forth ever so fluently, but applying the counsel to a specific is a different matter. A mother wants to know: "Shall I give consent for my sixteen-year-old daughter to go with this boy alone on dates? He is from a good family but from a different church. I am afraid if I say No that she will slip around and go anyway. I want to do the right for my daughter.

The real control must be built within. We can't begin too early to instill these principles and habits into mind, muscle, and emotion. But we can begin too late! First we must lead them to Christ. Then, who will feed and instruct Christ's young sheep? Who but godly parents and teachers and other Christian leaders?

Never answer a controversial question until you have prayed earnestly about it. Your teen will sense the serious import of your verdict if you ask him to give you time to think and pray over the problem first. You cannot expect a spur-of-the-moment answer to command the respect you wish from your teen. His questions deserve your most thoughtful and prayerful deliberation. Look into the youthful viewpoint; weigh carefully each alternative. Seek to understand New Testament guide rules through the help of Holy Spirit filled men and women.

Support and protect your teens with love, understanding, and trust, along with controls and disciplines. Help them *grow steady* before they go steady in serious dating. Help them acquire a standard of personal rightness and a standard by which to select a date who just may turn out to be a mate. This dating intelligence can be developed through wide dating experience— not *wild* dating, but selective dating of varied personalities.

SUMMING UP

What do your teens think about going steady?
What are your personal opinions?

At what age should fellows and girls get serious?
What is the best preparation for going steady?
Check the advantages of steady dating.
Check the drawbacks.
What are the variations of going steady?
What restrictions should parents make?
How can you balance trust and protection?

11

What Americans need in this sex-struck age is practical guidance rooted in firm moral principle. This is a mission that only the churches can perform properly. To do so, they must offer a cradle-to-the-grave . . .*

I'VE SLIPPED—WHO CAN I TALK TO?

Your Teens Say

"I am a boy fourteen years old. It may seem to you that I do not have enough faith in God, but I hope this isn't true. Recently a boy and girl were married—she hadn't even finished high school—the reason, she was going to have a baby. These were apparently good Christians, whose parents are leaders in the church. This makes me ask myself: Are none of us really good? Is our minister preaching to deaf ears? Is no one a true lover of Christ and his good way? Please, Verna, help restore my faith."

—Boy from the East

"In my early teens I associated with a bad crowd of young people. When I became a Christian I broke away from the old gang, but their influence had become a part of me. For some time I've been going with a nice Christian boy, but when I am around him I desire sex. When we kiss he holds me much too tight, and when we are alone on dates his hands never stay where they should. I am afraid my desires may get out of control. What can I do? Where will this lead? My church friends think I am wonderful, expect great things of me. I can't go to my pastor, for he knows me for what I am—a deceiver! Please help me!"

—Girl from the East

"Please help me. Help me find God! For two months I know he has been calling; I want to go to the altar, but I am too

*By Ed Kiester, from *Parade* Sunday Magazine, (October 1, 1961). Used by permission of Parade Publications, Inc.

frightened of the people watching. The burden of my sins is weighing me down. I have done little things like cheat and lie, but what is really tearing me down is something only God and I know. I want his pardon, but I do not feel it. I am only fifteen, but, Verna, I am already a prostitute. Please don't shame me now. I hate myself for it, and I haven't done anything wrong for quite a while. And I didn't take money. But I feel as if God could never forgive this sin. Please help me to find him, to know his tender love and guidance. I am going with a Christian boy who really loves and serves Christ in everything he does. But I don't deserve him. I'm a little no-good . . . Please help me! Pray for me."

—Girl from the Midwest

I can scarcely write for tears, for this is the last I've heard from the writer of the last letter. Can't we be more like Christ—hating the sin, yet loving the sinner? Who will leave the ninety-and-nine to go search and find and bring back this lamb who slipped from the fold? Will the church echo the welcome around the throne: "Rejoice, for the Lord brings back his own!"?

What about the pregnant bride? Can the church do less than extend full fellowship to these new homemakers in the spirit of forgiveness Christ offers to all who repent of their sins?

The lead quotation in this chapter is an excerpt from the article, "Is the Church Changing Its Mind About Sex?" Ed Kiester says that "churches of many hues and denominations have been shifting their ground on this most fundamental of moral questions." This does not mean that *chastity* is outmoded. It does mean exchange of "harshness and silence about sex" for education, counseling, and compassion.

In a recent conference at Green Lake, Wisconsin, more than five hundred clergymen spent five days discussing sex. One group declared that the church should "see itself as a redemptive fellowship—friendly, non-judgmental, forgiving, accepting. Re-examine the quality of its own interpersonal relationships. Seek and be ready to accept all people into fellowship, whatever they have done. Be compassionate, supportive, and empathetic."

When a girl has slipped, the next to the last person in the world she wants to face is her mother—last of all, her father. Picture if you can the girl's difficulty in finding any person at all to confide in, at least one who can give her understanding counsel. She needs help, encouragement to begin over—not upbraiding or blame. As the unfortunate girl wrote in her letter: "Please don't shame me; I hate myself."

Most urgent is the appeal: Save these young people who have made one misstep *before* they go deeper. Save those who desperately want to know how to recover.

A Misstep Need Not Be Fatal

Some mistakes are much more serious than others; some are permanent in their impact on personality and future relationships. But none need be fatal; God forgives, restores, and he redirects. He can and does fully save those who have been captivated by drink, drugs, or sex obsession—but not without sorrow, struggle, and persevering faith. Moreover, few are able to make the comeback without understanding, Christian help. Loving forgiveness may challenge the young sinner to a resurrection of good and noble desires and their fulfillment.

As much as we deplore the laxity of moral standards, we must admit that God forgives sins of sex, and so should we forgive, as fully as we hope to be forgiven of the sins we have committed.

With her permission, I want to share excerpts from letters of fourteen-year-old Harue (not her real name), with the earnest prayer that her experiences may provoke in concerned adults a more compassionate understanding and motivation to save other teens who have slipped.

"Dear Verna: "I will not tell you my age [later she told me] because you would be shocked. In the past I was a very good Christian, willing to give up anything for God, but things have changed. I've been going steady with a boy two years now, and I love him more than I do God. We plan to get married when we are old enough. I will try to tell you my main problem, hoping you will understand and help me. My problem is committing adultery; I have done this sin so many times I've stopped counting, though this boy is the only one I've given myself to.

"I am so under conviction I pray and cry for hours, but it seems I just can't reach God. I don't dare tell my mother; she is a good Christian and it would break her heart, and heaven only knows what she would do. I don't blame the Lord for not forgiving me; the first few times he did. Please tell me what to do and help me. God has refused me and will not listen to me any more. But I do want to be a good Christian and do God's will. P.S. I feel guilty for writing this letter; you are the only one who knows. Please tell me how I can control myself. Harue"

With all the persuasion I could prayerfully command I wrote this dear girl, pointing her to the only way of salvation. First, I called her attention to Christ's attitude to the woman taken in adultery (John 8:3-12). Christ did not condemn the woman; he saved her and said, "Go and sin no more." I urged Harue to face her problem squarely; then turn back to God and freedom in these few steps:

1. *Repent* today. Decide to give up this sin now—even if it breaks your heart. You and only you can make this decision. But the Holy Spirit stands near to help you turn around, to forsake sin and to face Christward. You can. (Rom. 10:9-11).

2. *Confess* the whole business to God—every thought, every feeling. Tell him how you love *sin* more than you love God—just as you told me—but that now you give it all up, regardless of how difficult it may be. (1 John 1:9).

3. *Believe* that God forgives, that he makes you clean, pure and free from all sin, that he saves you now. "Whosoever believeth on him shall not be ashamed" (Rom. 10:11). God keeps his promises; you can depend on that. No matter how heavy your heart still feels, just believe God. Joy will come, peace will flood your soul like a river, washing away those awful feelings of guilt.

4. *Forgive yourself.* You'll never know perfect peace until you turn loose the past and forgive your own failings. You cannot go back and change one single hour, but glorious thought! God wipes the slate clean! You are now his child, just as though you had never failed him. He has removed your sins as far as the East is from the West, to remember them against you nevermore. (Ps. 103:12).

What of the Future?

Stay away from temptation. This is the test. The devil is not ready to give you up; he will tempt you harder than ever. Old impulses, emotions, desires—they will flood your being, but these are not your master. God is in control; look quickly to him in prayer. Resist the devil and he will flee from you every time. God is with you in this fight. Stay with God and he will stay with you; together you will win.

Pray, watch, and *work.*

Do not date singly, not for a long time. This is not going to be easy. You have disturbed emotions and physical faculties which God has reserved for marriage partners only. Now you must get these emotions back under control. Place them under the control of God's Holy Spirit, and cooperate with him. Your part is to stay away from temptation. Petting and kissing is out; don't take any risks.

I requested Harue to make three promises to me as follows:

1. I promise to repent, confess, believe, and accept Christ on his terms at once.

2. I promise to try to avoid situations which might lead back to wrongdoing.

3. I promise that if I should happen to slip or fail, I will call for help at once—ask God's forgiveness and seek counsel from my pastor or write and tell you. This is our agreement.

Soon the girl wrote:

"Dear Verna, God did speak to me quite clearly through your letter, which I have read about twenty times. At first I was stunned, for no one has ever put it to me in such true words. I started crying and fell to my knees. You see I was saved when quite young, but backslid and went into this deep sin when I was in the seventh grade. Your letter has made me believe with all my heart. Yes, Verna, I am at the crossroads and I have already crossed. I praise God with all my heart for putting his words into your mouth. Please keep talking to me and keep on praying for me.

I love you too, Harue"

Months passed before Harue was able to break away completely from this boy. At first she had hopes that he too would become a Christian and that they would marry when older. But when it became evident that he would not share her new life in Christ, she gave up going with him. About seven months after she had first written me—with many letters between—she wrote this:

"Dear Verna: I am making more good grades in school than I ever have before. . . . The other evening ——— came to see me, the first time since we broke up. He wants me to go back to him, but I told him no, that God's will is going to be done. He is so lost, and I do feel sorry for him. This may sound cruel, but I

78

really can't stand to be around him any more. The sight of him makes me sick; I don't have the least bit of love for him.

Love you, Harue"

The next letter was full of school news and church activities and: "The Lord has blessed me greatly. I thank you for your prayers. I try to make sure that everything I do pleases God, and I know that he is my Savior. Please continue to pray that I will always do God's will.

Love you too, Harue"

It was not easy; Harue did have a terrific struggle, but she kept to our agreement all the way. And I am happy to report that this girl has made a remarkable recovery. I give her credit for unusual strength of character and purpose, which though crushed, refused to be destroyed. Through redeeming love and grace, the future again holds promise of a good and happy life.

Summing Up

Encourage your church to launch a program emphasizing these points:

1. Counseling for the married and for the engaged.

2. Sex education for the young and their parents.

3. More consideration and compassion for those who have slipped or who have fallen into various entanglements.

Keep on the coattails of youth who are beginning to stray.

Parents of one who has slipped: Put away your own shame and grief. Restore your child with love and acceptance.

12

Young love-making, that gossamer web! Even the point it clings to—the things whence its subtle interlacings are swung—are scarcely perceptible: momentary touches of finger-tips, meetings of rays from blue and dark orbs, unfinished phrases, lightest changes of cheek and lip, faintest tremors.—George Eliot

HOW CAN I EXPRESS AFFECTION?

Your Teens Say

"I know that when you are growing up you face new problems, but I just don't know about this one, whether or not it is wrong. I have been going with a very nice boy for some time, and I have always tried to act as a Christian should—and I have. But lately we have stopped after a date and talked and kissed once or twice, never anything but kiss. When I am doing this I feel that it is all right, but afterward I wonder if it is. I have prayed about it but don't seem to get an answer. Please help me to know what I should do. I love the Lord with all my heart."

—Christian Girl

"So far I have been very fortunate about temptations most teen-agers face. I've never had an urge to smoke or drink; such things are revolting! But even kids whom I considered Christians now find these things fun. They sneak behind their parents' back to do things I have been taught are wrong. Now I find there are no decent trustworthy boys in our youth group. I've been told this problem would arise sometime in my teens. It has, and I am a very lonesome girl, and I find myself thinking that even a necking date is better than no date at all. And yet I really don't want the kind of friends that necking would bring. I am sure there must be decent boys around, but if I don't find them at church, where can I find them?"

—Lonesome Girl

"The adults wonder why I don't date some of the girls whom they consider wonderful. I want a nice, clean Christian girl very, very much, but I just don't know where to find one. My parents keep saying the right one will come along, but the reverse seems to happen. Should a fellow let down his standards some, or just what should he do?"

—Lonesome Boy

"It is hard for me to avoid temptation when I am with a certain boy. He says he can't understand why I won't park with him, but all he wants to do when we are alone is neck, and I know what that leads to. I don't want to offend him, but, Verna, I'm afraid to keep going with him. I'm afraid I haven't enough strength to overcome."

—Bewildered Girl

Just What Is Petting?

Any lovemaking which is sexually exciting, we call *petting*. It can be kissing, caressing, or fondling; but regardless of how it begins, petting is always progressive. In other words, the greatest danger in petting is the compulsion to continue until all controls are gone.

When you say to your teens, "You must not pet!" be very sure they know just what you are talking about and why. William Genné, a leading church authority on family life, made this statement: "The churches have a compelling duty to provide an understanding of the true nature of sex, its goodness, its means of fulfillment, and its role in the Christian life. Many churches have taken remarkable steps toward achieving this goal."

This comes from a Lutheran publication: "Most social scientists realize that biological facts are ineffective without a spiritual sense of values and Christian attitudes. . . . This is a big, new task for the church."

Part of this task is a program of sex education for parents. Mothers and fathers know something of the risks and dangers their teens face in an age of "dating freedom" unmatched in civilized society. But few parents know what to do about it or how to give satisfying answers when teens seek information. Young people feel either too restricted or too unprotected. We must give them a safe period to grow into the maturity they covet. We must give them a loving climate of trust, understanding, and limited freedom.

81

Teach your teens that the car is no place to kiss if they are going to kiss good-night. Neither is it best to park and talk. The practice definitely encourages intimacies, and it invites suspicion from onlookers. Encourage the young people to bring their dates home and give them a corner where they can talk without too much interference from the younger clan or adults. Be extra firm in the rule: "No parties without parents!"

Mothers of little ones sigh for the years when their toddlers will be teen-agers—then they will have time for all those outside activities! All too soon it happens. No more noses to wipe, ears to wash, buttons to button, prayers to be heard. Then Mom learns the truth: responsibility has doubled. Teens are different, but far more demanding of intelligent attention than babies ever were. If only Mom could fully appreciate how much they need her now, need her love, her sympathetic interest, her wise restraint, her glad approval. Tomorrow, all this will change.

How can a mother relax contentedly watching television, knowing that her teen-age daughter is parked out front beside an ardent lover—for hours? When one father complained about such a situation, his wife rejoined: "Can't you remember when we were young?" He answered quietly, "That's the trouble; I am remembering."

But How Can Youth Express Love?

A girl of fifteen was going steady with a boy, seventeen. One evening when he was helping her with her algebra, the mother coming upon them was shocked to find her daughter calmly sitting upon the young man's lap. "That is not proper," the mother reprimanded later. "A girl does not sit on a boy's lap."

"But, Mother, we were not doing anything wrong," the girl said in a grieved tone. "If you think we're so bad, you ought to see how other couples act."

We might as well acknowledge that most of our teaching is negative: don't neck, don't pet, don't park, don't get too intimate. "Tell us plainly what we *can* do that will be proper and safe." But that is not so smooth and easy when we have harped on the "don'ts" so long. For the most part, young dating couples should be content just to be together, once in a while holding hands, and on special occasions perhaps a good-night kiss between special friends.

Contrary to almost universal indulgence, the church must

82

teach that physical expression of love is a most dangerous pastime for the unmarried, especially for teen daters. Just this week a young girl wants to know how she can overcome shyness. "Everybody in our crowd necks, all but me. I want a boy to kiss me, but when he tries I freeze up. When a boy put his head on my shoulder, guess what I said? 'I'm not that sort of girl!' Now wasn't I stupid? If I can't overcome this, my life is nothing."

Shall we teach our teens to break down these protective reserves which are built into their better selves? If so, we can encourage beauty contests; we can send them to schools for models or special charm schools. They may even make Hollywood. Or shall we persist in discovering ways to glorify again the virtues which our society once revered? Picture the delightful contrast; television and daily papers giving the limelight to goodness, nobleness, chastity, fortitude. How refreshing to hear more about marriages that do not blow apart in the first ill wind, and about juvenile worthies who stand pat on honor and duty and faithfulness. And wouldn't we be glad if this better side of America sounded forth on the screens of our faraway neighbors, who now see us as a whole nation engrossed with money, violence, and sex?

Our own youngsters are fed up with this distasteful picture too. Positive teaching and preaching attract and challenge girls and boys in our homes and churches. "How-to" instead of "how-not-to" stimulates their eager young hearts and minds to positive thinking and acting.

Affection Between More Serious Daters

The young adults who are looking forward to marriage in the not-too-distant future, rightly wish to reveal their love. But how? Not in any manner which will cheapen that love or lessen respect. For the most part, physical expression must still wait. There are innumerable ways, tender and thoughtful, of saying, I love you. Grandparents recall the poem beginning, "Still sits the schoolhouse by the road, A ragged beggar sunning . . ." And the spelling bee where the maiden said: "I'm sorry that I spelt the word; I hate to go above you—The brown eyes lowered still, Because, because you see, I love you."

Each may express affection in thoughtful gestures for the other's comfort and well-being. A girl delights in preparing dinner for her lover; he may spend Saturday helping her refinish an antique or make a frame for her painting. It's heaven to work out a problem together. Hours slip by while they draw up plans for a dream house. Parents may help devise activities which divert the lovers from too close engrossment with each other.

Even the engaged couple need guidance and restraint. Those more experienced must teach youth self-control. Chastity is still up-to-date; therefore, lovemaking must be kept within prudent and comfortable bounds. How far is too far? That is a question youth often ask. When excited sex emotions have usurped the place of tender and light caresses, lovers have ignored safety signals. When they have lost interest in all the things they used to enjoy together, contriving to spend every moment alone making love—high time to call a halt. The two had better discipline their emotions and get back on a more level keel.

When a girl gives herself unreservedly to her sweetheart, she forfeits the exquisite pleasure of one day giving herself to her husband as she would wish. She loses that special pride and precious dream of coming to her true love in all her virgin sweetness. The same ideal holds true for the man. It is always a tragedy when lovers fritter away an experience which God intended to be a "Symbol of love, control, and mastery."

Let's teach our youth the sacredness of God's law of love, "Thou shalt not commit adultery."

Youth Counselor Says

"In working with and observing youth in two states, my deep concern has been the conduct of sweethearts. My young people love me, invite me to everything they plan, respect me too; yet I find it next to impossible to approach them on this subject. It is sweet to see them holding hands or walk arm-in-arm, but to embrace and kiss at their gatherings is, in my opinion, undesirable conduct. The engaged should restrain themselves, as well as those who are only sweethearts. I do not consider myself a 'wet blanket' or a gripe, but I fear that this problem may be more serious than we realize."

Who will approach our young Christians with a challenge to the highest goals of discipline and dedication in our society? All concerned adults need expert knowledge to be able to work intelligently with youth. Fortunately, this is within reach of each of us, if we will take time for reading and research. Young people welcome frank discussions on down-to-earth situations. In the heart of every sincere young Christian there is the incessant desire for learning and growth in mind and spirit. There must be constant reexamining and reshaping of attitudes and actions. The approach we make must not be condemnatory, but rather, trustful, loving, supportive, and informative. At special gatherings, a group will quickly abandon fun activities to join in a friendly jam session. When one or two real puzzlers are thrown into open debate, the young people themselves often come up with good sound solutions.

This applies to special convocations of youth—retreats, camps, conventions—where a few, clear, reasonable rules are imperative. Given a chance, the youth group will mark out the most essential regulations. Without these guides, there is always the fringe handful who add the wrong flavor to any gathering of young people. Some few may even run into quite serious trouble.

Adults who have been taught (and who teach) ordinary rules of propriety, take it for granted that teens away from home know what is expected of them. Many do not know. One consultant at a convention was surprised when she came upon a young couple in the girl's hotel room, sitting on the bed watching television. No wrong was intended. But we know the danger of ignoring common rules of propriety.

Family camps afford ideal opportunities for closer understanding between parents and their youth. The idea of family camps is growing by leaps and bounds among many church groups. Nature's outdoors encourages reflection and discussion of matters of intimate concern in a frank and religious atmosphere.

The Task Is Yours

Parents and Church, there's no one but you to guide youth through happy but danger-frought dating years. The task is yours to prepare youth for the total expression of love and unselfish affection in Christian marriage, home, and family.

SUMMING UP

How can you discover your teens most intimate problems? How can you lessen risky situations?

85

How can very young lovers express affection?

What *don'ts* would you suggest?

What *dos* can you safely offer?

Be specific: just what can they *do?*

How can serious lovers express affection?

Are time and place relevant?

How far is too far?

How should engaged couples occupy their time alone?

For youth camps, conventions, and other such church gatherings, what protective rules do you suggest? Who should make them?

How can we prepare youth for engagement?

How can we prepare youth for marriage?

13

It is noted that (1) an increasing number [of young people] want to know the meaning of religion, (2) the majority of all ages have as a problem that of getting help on religious problems, yet (3) an increasing number dislike church service . . . but the dissatisfaction apparently does not grow out of disinterest; rather it grows out of felt needs that are not being met.*

HOW CAN WE KNOW GOD . . . ?

Your Teens Say

"How can we really know there is a God? How can we know the Bible is God's word? Couldn't this just be a book someone has written about a person called God? Many times I have tried to be a Christian, but each time I have failed, because I can't see or hear God. Please try to help me if you can soon; I've nearly given up."

—No Name

"Deep in my heart I believe there is a God, but I can't prove it to myself. Now if I feel this way, can I still be saved? Should I be absolutely sure there is a God? How will I know that I will stay with Christianity? Does anyone ever really know?"

"Once in my Sunday school class I felt that I should get saved right then, but I wanted to wait. Was I sinning? Will God still save me if I ask him to?"

"How do we know that the Bible is meant for us today? It seems to be talking to people back in those days. How do we know that no mistakes were made when the Bible was written? I really hate to bother you so much, but it seems that more and more questions pile up. They are so complicated that I feel like no one can ever answer them. Could you give me some Scripture passages that will show me for sure that I can be saved?"

*Kuhlen, p. 449.

In a recent international youth convention at Houston, Texas, senior highs wrote their most urgent questions on slips of paper. These are typical:

Is a secret longing the first step toward knowing God?

Can we know God's love?

Can we know God when very young? Is there a difference when we are more mature?

How far must you go really to know God?

How does God speak to us?

Can a Christian know God's voice?

Can you love God and listen to "Rock'n'Roll"?

Is it possible to know God to the fullest extent?

Do *you* know God?

Can You Produce Evidences?

Youth will accept no sham, no shallow, superficial religion. The most critically convincing evidence a witness for Christ can present is a personal acquaintance with Christ. The evidences are affirmed in the glow of a Christian's countenance, the qualities and attitudes of his spirit, and the outward expression—in actions and reactions. This assurance stems from a climactic encounter with God in Christ, confirmed by the Holy Spirit and subsequent growth in Christlikeness, in grace, and in knowledge.

The proofs of God, the Bible and Christianity, are found in living examples. You are the evidences that God is, that the Bible is true, that Christ is Savior and Lord. "Ye are my witnesses, saith the Lord, and my servants whom I have chosen: that ye may know and believe me, and understand that I am he: before me there was no God formed, neither shall there be after me. I, even I, am the Lord; and beside me there is no savior. I have declared, and have saved, and I have showed . . . therefore ye are my witnesses, saith the Lord, that I am God" (Isa. 43:10-12).

Is It True?

The lead quotation at the beginning of this chapter refers to an extensive survey of young people in Maryland. Is it true that the majority of youth experience difficulty in getting help on religious problems? Does their apparent lack of interest indicate that the church is failing to meet their needs?

In spite of the upsurge of religious interest in America, "35 million boys and girls under 17 still never attend church school," says Carl F. H. Henry, editor of *Christianity Today*.

In *Christian Herald's* "Sunday School Teacher," a young adult says "I don't like Sunday school." He says teaching is too shallow, repetition of the same stuff is deadly, science and the Bible are never brought together, teachers have not figured out answers for themselves. "My friend who is an atheist asks me questions I can't answer. I'm going to figure out answers to satisfy me. But I wish Sunday school had given me a little more help."

What Can the Church Do?

Ronald C. Doll, in *Christianity Today*, February 27, 1961, says that the most critical issues cluster about the following:

1. Vitalize and apply the Christian message to daily lives.

2. Select curriculum content that creates greatest behavioral effect.

3. Recruit able, basically qualified teachers.

4. Provide in-service growth for teachers—as to instructional competence and spiritual discernment.

"They Would See Jesus" titles an article by Catherine Marshall in *Christian Herald*, August, 1960. Here are a few of her most provocative points: Add your own experience to the Sunday school lesson, admit into the session more of the presence and direction of the Holy Spirit, introduce youth to Jesus Christ. She says that young people always want to know more about "how you met Christ" and "how can you be so sure Jesus is alive?"

"Teach the Bible as series of stories," Catherine Marshall urges. "One remembers a story . . . it's the most important single discovery for writing and speaking I ever made." Catherine's brother, Bob Wood, teaches pre-teen boys—with great success. He says the boys are quick to detect hypocrisy. Teach them to apply Christianity and discuss issues of the day. And, as Bob Wood exemplifies, become their friend, if you would win them to Christ.

From the reports of successful teachers, it appears that loving Christ and his young people is more important than knowing the lesson. When they meet the Master, they will know that Christ is the answer; no other will satisfy.

What Can Parents Do?

Parents can take more interest in the questions of their children, from toddlers on up. They can encourage friendly discussion of problems of the individual, the family, and the world. They can bring the Bible up-to-date in the day-to-day experiences of family living and in the relationships outside the home.

Parents can make Christ so much a part of family life Monday through Saturday, that Sunday with its worship, fellowship, study, and sermon will be a happy and natural beginning of every week. Parents can make Christ known early to their children through their own vibrant relationship with him as Savior, Shepherd, Healer, and ever-present Guest.

We must be specific, as the following letter indicates:

"Dear Verna, Must I accept the Christian way of life simply because my parents have taught me that this is the only way to God? When I was a child, I swallowed all this—never questioning the truth of my mother's faith nor my father's belief nor that of my Sunday school teacher and pastor. But now that I am a senior in high school, I wonder about all this. Does not every one have a right to his own ideas of what is really truth? Suppose I had been born into a Muslim home? or a Jewish? These people also believe in one God.

"How do we know the Bible is true? Just because my father told me, and his father told him? Sorry, but that's not enough for me. If I am going to stake my life and the future one on some belief, I must know it firsthand for myself. That's why I say I'm searching for the truth. Yes, searching, searching . . . but finding no answers. I don't know which way to turn, and yet I do believe there is a God. If only I knew where and how to find him! Do you think there is hope for me?"

—Confused Girl

I wrote the girl: "There is hope, for you say that you do believe. And Jesus said, 'For every one who asks receives, and he who seeks finds. . . .' Man could not scale the long heights up to God, so: God came down!" I went on to tell about a small group of Christians on tour in Egypt. As the young Muslim guide conducted the group through the Citadel of Saladin in

90

Cairo, he proudly displayed the glory of the ancient mosques. But the Christians were deeply touched by the sight of Muslims calling on their god, Allah, who seemed so far away.

The young guide said, "We all seek the same God. You Christians call him God; we call him Allah. You follow his prophet Jesus; we follow his prophet Mohammed. It's all the same thing."

One Christian had the courage to speak up: "No, Abou, it is not the same; Christians do not follow Jesus as a prophet. We believe *Allah* himself came down to man! God came to earth as a man, lived and suffered and died for the sins of the world, and rose again. Jesus was his name."

The young Muslim was first shocked, then amazed at such an incredible idea. Throughout the day he approached other Christians, and all gave the same answer: "Yes, God came down to man." Late that evening Abou said, "It is the most wonderful thought I've ever heard of. If only it could be true!"

The girl was right in wanting to know for herself, for a secondhand experience will not satisfy. But she was seeking for a theory, a truth—something abstract, unless associated with something or someone substantial. We can find the answer only in a person. That Person is Christ. Robert Browning expressed the thought in "A Death in the Desert":

> I say, the acknowledgment of God in Christ
> Accepted by thy reason, solves for thee
> All questions in the earth and out of it. . . .

What Is Truth?

Ask not *what* but *who; who* is truth? When Pilate asked Jesus, "Are you a king?" Jesus replied: " 'For this I was born, and for this I have come into the world, to bear witness to the truth. . . .' Pilate said to him, 'What is truth?' " (John 18:37-38*).

Jesus gave the answer to Thomas on the long night before His crucifixion. "Thomas said to him, 'Lord, we do not know where you are going; how can we know the way?' Jesus said to him, 'I am the way, and the truth, and the life; no one comes to the Father, but by me. If you had known me, you would have known my Father also . . .' " (John 14:5-7*).

How Can We Know the Bible Is True?

"You search the scriptures, because you think that in them you have eternal life; and it is they that bear witness to me;

yet you refuse to come unto me that you may have life" (John 5:39-40). These words refer, of course, to the Old Testament Scriptures, because the New had not been written at this time. But the questions I wish to ask are these: How did Christ regard the Scriptures? Did he accept the Bible as the inspired word of God? We can answer assuredly: Jesus believed the Scriptures; Jesus obeyed and fulfilled them.

1. Jesus Believed the Scriptures

"If you believed Moses, you would believe me, for he wrote of me" (John 5:45-46*). On the night of the Last Supper, Jesus said to his disciples: "You will all fall away; for it is written, 'I will strike the shepherd, and the sheep will be scattered'" (Mark 14:27*). Jesus believed the prophecy which is found in Zechariah 13:7.

After the Resurrection, when Jesus joined the two disciples on the road to Emmaus, he said: "'O foolish men, and slow of heart to believe all that the prophets have spoken! Was it not necessary that Christ should suffer these things and enter into his glory? And beginning with Moses and all the prophets, he interpreted to them in all the scriptures the things concerning himself'" (Luke 24:25-27*).

2. Jesus Obeyed and Fulfilled the Scriptures

As the promised King and Messiah and the Suffering Servant of the Old Testament prophecy, Jesus was determined to fulfill to the letter all that was written of him. "'Behold, we are going up to Jerusalem, and everything that is written of the Son of man by the prophets will be accomplished'" (Luke 18:31*).

Jesus was obedient; he willingly took the road which he knew was leading to suffering and death. When Peter attempted to fight for him, Jesus forbade him, saying: "'How then should the scriptures be fulfilled, that it must be so?'" (Matt. 26:54*). Christ's life on earth began with the fulfillment of the prophecy concerning his birth by a virgin (see Matthew 1:22-23). Notice that this was spoken *of the Lord* by the prophet: "that it might be fulfilled . . . Out of Egypt have I called my Son. . . . And he came and dwelt in a city called Nazareth: that it might be fulfilled . . ." (Matt. 2:14, 23). And on and on throughout the Gospels and the other writings of the New Testament!

All the predictions, claims, descriptions pointing to the Messiah—all were supremely enacted in the life and death and resurrection of our Lord. Beyond doubt, Christ believed the Scriptures as the divinely inspired word of God; he quoted them freely, obeyed them, and fulfilled them to the letter. If we believe in Christ, we believe the Bible.

The "Christ Way" Works

While on earth Christ definitely proved his claims as the divine Son of God. But if his works had ended there, we might have thought of him as only one other great man, or even as the most perfect man who ever lived. But that was only the beginning. Christ enters again and again into human experience; God comes down and lives in each person who will receive him as Savior and Lord. For there is no other *name*, no other way to God and salvation.

The "Christ way" has worked in millions of lives; the miracle of transformation happens over and over in the most hopeless of sinners, as it happens also in the hearts of those who receive Him in early youth. And millions have believed in Christ so utterly as to suffer martyrdom rather than renounce their Lord. No other person has ever made such claims or held out such guarantees: a new birth for all who will repent, confess, and forsake sins and believe (John 3:3, 16-18), power to live the new life and do the works which he did, eternal blessedness after this. No other pledges to come live in one's very being as Sanctifier, Comforter, Teacher, and Guide.

How Can I Find Him?

Stop! Listen. Let God find you. "Behold, I stand at the door and knock; if any one hears my voice and opens the door, I will come in to him and eat with him, and he with me" (Rev. 3:20*).

In the quiet of your soul, call to him, "Lord, I repent of my sins; please forgive—take away my doubts and fears. I surrender them all. I now open wide my heart's door. Stand no longer outside, Lord. I need You, I want You more than all else. Come in, for I do now accept You as my Lord and Savior."

Just hold this thought, this confession, until your whole soul fully agrees in perfect faith—until the Spirit brings a response of acceptance—joy and peace and assurance! You may feel nothing at first, but wait for this; it will not fail. The answer will come.

Christ stands outside waiting. It's your move.

The above is the gist of my letter to "Confused Girl."

Religious Confusion

Youth want to know the answer to many other questions: Why so many Christian denominations? Which church is right? Shouldn't all Christians work together? How can I promote the cause of Christian brotherhood? What can Christians do to oppose communism?

Reasonable questions, but not easy to answer. The desire for Christian unity is gathering momentum, as evidenced by the dreams and plans for mergers among various religious bodies. The biblical ideal is timely: "Endeavoring to keep the unity of the Spirit in the bond of peace. Till we all come in the unity of the faith, and of the knowledge of the Son of God, unto a perfect man, unto the measure of the stature of the fullness of Christ" (Eph. 4:3, 13).

"There is more open and aggressive atheism than at any other point of human history," says Archbishop Garbett. Modern science and modern philosophy are for the most part either antagonistic or indifferent to the Christian faith. Much of this unbelief—denials of eternal verities—has infiltrated and weakened the church. Yet, when the first atom bomb was exploded, Dr. Compton said: "Now we know there is a God."

Against this alarming growth of skepticism, Wilbur M. Smith, Professor of English Bible at Fuller Theological Seminary, suggests only one hope, and that is "a return to, a full confidence in, and a loving obedience to, the Holy Scriptures."

A layman from Lebanon, and former President of the United Nations General Assembly, is Charles Malik. Recently in an interview, Dr. Malik was questioned concerning the hope of Christianity's witness against the Communist threat. Dr. Malik's answer is significant. He says that the most important thing is "ardent prayer for the Holy Spirit to come mightily into hearts of men. . . . Do you think that mass organization without the inclusion of the Holy Spirit, . . . can withstand the smash of the Communist offensive? Not at all!"

While Dr. Malik believes that in the field of Christian unity there are signs of great hope, still he points out evident weaknesses of professed Christians—softheaded, too worldly, not speaking with conviction.

What Shall Be Our Answer?

Your teens are asking—and they have a right to ask—to question and examine every doctrine, every practice, every procedure, every ideal which we press upon them. Youth want to know the truth. Not *what*, but *who* is the answer? We know if we know Christ. Teens look to parents, teachers, pastors—to all Christian adults to help them discover anew the verities of old. Urgently and earnestly, let us look to the Holy Spirit to lead us that we may lead youth—to Christ who is the answer.

SUMMING UP

What do *your* teens want to know?

Do you listen to them with genuine interest?

Is your church meeting needs of youth?

How do you rate as a church school teacher?

Do you have a real sense of purpose?

Do you know the lesson content?

Do you get it across?

Do you encourage participation?

Do you encourage "skeptical" questions?

Do you apply lessons to youth life?

Are you humble?

Do you give encouragement, appreciation, and weekday attention?

Do your teens know Christ?

Do you know Him?

Do you really care—enough to make Him known?

In your opinion, what are the five most important questions which your teens ask?

What are your answers?